Health and Political Engagement

Social scientists have only recently begun to explore the link between health and political engagement. Understanding this relationship is vitally important from both a scholarly and a policy-making perspective.

This book is the first to offer a comprehensive account of health and political engagement. Using both individual-level and country-level data drawn from the European Social Survey, World Values Survey and new Finnish survey data, it provides an extensive analysis of how health and political engagement are connected. It measures the impact of various health factors on a wide range of forms of political engagement and attitudes and helps shed light on the mechanisms behind the interaction between health and political engagement.

This text is of key interest scholars, students and policy-makers in health, politics, and democracy, and more broadly in the social and health and medical sciences.

Mikko Mattila is Professor of Political Science at the University of Helsinki, Finland. He is the Head of the Academy of Finland funded research project 'Health and Political Engagement'.

Lauri Rapeli is Acting Director of the Social Science Research Institute at the Åbo Akademi University, Finland. He is a member of the Academy of Finland funded research project 'Health and Political Engagement'.

Hanna Wass is Academy Research Fellow in the Department of Political and Economic Studies at the University of Helsinki, Finland. She is a member of the Academy of Finland funded research project 'Health and Political Engagement'.

Peter Söderlund is Adjunct Professor of Political Science and an Academy Research Fellow in the Social Science Research Institute at Åbo Akademi University, Finland. He is a member of the Academy of Finland funded research project 'Health and Political Engagement'.

Routledge Research in Comparative Politics

For a full list of titles, please visit: www.routledge.com/Routledge-Research-in-Comparative-Politics/book-series/CP

Health and Political Engagement

Mikko Mattila, Lauri Rapeli, Hanna Wass and Peter Söderlund

Routledge
Taylor & Francis Group
LONDON AND NEW YORK

First published 2018
by Routledge
2 Park Square, Milton Park, Abingdon, Oxon OX14 4RN

and by Routledge
711 Third Avenue, New York, NY 10017

Routledge is an imprint of the Taylor & Francis Group, an informa business

British Library Cataloguing-in-Publication Data
A catalogue record for this book is available from the British Library

Library of Congress Cataloging-in-Publication Data
Names: Mattila, Mikko, author. | Rapeli, Lauri, author. | Wass, Hanna,
    author. | Sèoderlund, Peter, 1976– author.
Title: Health and political engagement / Mikko Mattila, Lauri Rapeli,
    Hanna Wass and Peter Sèoderlund.
Other titles: Routledge research in comparative politics ; 73.
Description: Abingdon, Oxon ; New York, NY : Routledge, 2018. |
    Series: Routledge research in comparative politics ; 73 | Includes
bibliographical references and index.
Identifiers: LCCN 2017010975 | ISBN 9781138673809 (hardback) |
    ISBN 9781315561691 (ebook)
Subjects: MESH: Health Policy | Politics | Social Theory
Classification: LCC RA425 | NLM WA 525 | DDC 362.1—dc23
LC record available at https://lccn.loc.gov/2017010975

ISBN: 978-1-138-67380-9 (hbk)
ISBN: 978-0-367-87843-6 (pbk)

Typeset in Times New Roman
by Apex CoVantage, LLC

Contents

Figures

Tables

Foreword

This book is the product of the research project 'Health and Political Engagement', financed by the Academy of Finland between 2013 and 2017 (project numbers 266844 and 273433). The project has been led by Mikko Mattila, and the other authors of this book have formed the core of the research team.

When preparing the grant application for the project and writing the first manuscripts on health and political engagement in 2012, a new wave of studies on the subject had recently been published. An increasing number of political scientists started turning to personal health for a fresh perspective on the determinants of political engagement. In this book, we offer a comprehensive account on the subject.

During multiple conversations, both within our group and with colleagues home and abroad, we gained a mutual understanding on how to participate in the ongoing scholarly debate. First and foremost, we felt there was a need in the literature for a presentation of different aspects in the relationship between personal health and political engagement. Journal articles alone would not be enough, because they are inevitably short and do not allow the authors to consider more than only a few issues at a time.

So writing a book that would discuss various aspects of both health and engagement from different theoretical angles seemed like a good idea. As in every project, many other actors play an important role besides the authors. We thank the Academy of Finland and the Finnish Cultural Foundation for financing our project. Hannu Lahtinen, Pekka Martikainen, Achillefs Papageorgiou and Reijo Sund from the University of Helsinki were invaluable partners in planning the survey used in this book and developing ideas through collaboration in authoring various articles. André Blais from Université de Montrèal and Elisabeth Gidengil and Dietlind Stolle from McGill University have been involved in many ways, for which we like to express our gratitude. Christopher Ojeda, Julie Pacheco and Lisa Schur have also offered their expertise on various occasions. Henrik Oscarsson from the University of Gothenburg hosted Lauri Rapeli's visit, during which also Elina Lindgren, Mikael Persson and Maria Solevid kindly offered their comments on our theoretical framework. We thank you all!

1 Introduction

Health and political engagement

There is a growing recognition that "health and illness shape who we are politically" (Carpenter, 2012, p. 303). The relationship between health and political behaviour is vitally important from both a scholarly and a policymaking perspective, and yet the topic has typically attracted more attention from scholars working in health-related fields than from political scientists.

This book is the first attempt by political scientists to offer a comprehensive account of how personal health and political engagement are related. It is arguably a timely contribution to the extensive body of literature on political participation, ideological orientations and vote choice. Although a vast amount of research has shown that engagement in politics is strongly connected to socio-economic status, as well as psychological factors, only a few studies have focused on the role of health (Smets and van Ham, 2013). In this book, we review previous research to establish the state of the art regarding this discipline, as well as conduct extensive empirical analyses concerning health and political engagement. On the basis of a solid theoretical framework, we test several hypotheses in order to understand the mechanisms contributing to the association between health and political engagement. We also look at how the association between health and engagement is affected by contextual factors, along with examining the political representation of people in poor health.

Considering health as a predictor of various aspects of political engagement is not entirely new as an idea (for a review, see Blank and Hines, 2001, pp. 91–3; Peterson, 1990, pp. 82–6), but social scientists have only recently begun to explore the connections with growing enthusiasm. There are several plausible reasons for such a rise in scholarly interest in the subject. Most noteworthy is the fact that health status has a considerable direct impact on the problem of political inequality. Health disparities are a major contemporary issue in many Western democracies. Differences in personal health and well-being are increasing, even in established welfare states such as the Nordic countries (OECD, 2015). As people are nowadays living longer than ever before, the proportion of pensioners is increasing. As a consequence, the number of citizens whose political behaviour could be affected by health problems is also growing. Health disparities are therefore likely to translate into unequal political participation in Western democracies.

The book is aimed at a broad spectrum of readers: scholars, students and policymakers with a professional interest in health, politics and equal opportunities for democratic citizenship. It will be useful as a textbook, as well as a handbook for anyone interested in fields such as political science, sociology, social medicine, social capital, nursing and health sciences. Our overarching theme is political equality. We show that poor health can influence an individual's resources and motivation for political engagement through multiple channels. Understanding the link between these two not only increases our knowledge of the mechanisms of political behaviour but helps to promote more inclusive democratic processes.

Health and inequality

Over the past decade, several influential studies have identified growing inequality as one of the urgent risks faced by contemporary societies (e.g., Atkinson, 2015; Dorling, 2014, 2015; Jensen and van Kersbergen, 2017; Galbraith, 2016; Grusky and Kricheli-Katz, 2012; Marmot, 2015; Putnam, 2015; Savage, 2015; Stiglitz, 2012; Therborn, 2013; Wilkinson and Pickett, 2009). This applies particularly to market-liberalist countries, such as the US, where income heavily differentiates various opportunities and outcomes (Enns, 2015, p. 1060). Although inequality has been less pronounced in the Nordic welfare states, which are traditionally characterized by progressive taxation and extensive redistribution, a recent OECD report (2015) reveals that income inequality has also risen in Sweden, Finland, Norway and Denmark since the mid-1980s. However, from a comparative perspective, income disparities are still relatively modest in these countries.

Health is an important component in terms of both illustrating and contributing to inequalities. In their often-cited comparative study, Wilkinson and Pickett (2010) showed that health and various types of social problems were related to income inequality in rich countries (see also Hiilamo and Kangas, 2014; Pickett and Wilkinson, 2015). This association suggests that inequality harms everyone's health, not just those living in poverty. The potential path between the two is complex: income differences may increase social distances, which accentuate status differences, which in turn increase status competition, social evaluation anxiety and lower self-esteem, which is harmful for all social groups (Jensen and van Kersbergen, 2017, p. 26). The same holds at the individual level, which can be best captured by the concept of 'social gradient'. The link between socio-economic status and health not only concerns those in poverty but all citizens: the lower a person's socio-economic status, the worse his/her health (Marmot, 2015, p. 15).

Economic inequality is reflected in social inequality; in turn, these two forms of inequality jointly affect political engagement and representation. Political participation is affected by a person's overall level of well-being, social networks and life situation. While this is particularly evident when it comes to voting, socio-economic factors also increase the likelihood that a person will become involved in other forms of participation, such as taking part in demonstrations and signing petitions. These factors also affect a person's sense of political agency, political interest and political knowledge, the attention he/she pays to electoral campaigns and the trust he/she has in political institutions (see e.g., Grönlund and Wass eds., 2016). In terms of representation, the results from the US, where the issue has been extensively addressed at an empirical level, are depressing. As Gilens (2015, p. 1070) summarizes: "Of course, affluent Americans do not always get the policies they prefer either. But the affluent are twice as likely to see the policies they strongly favor adopted, while the policies they strongly oppose are only one-fifth as likely to be adopted as those that are strongly opposed by the middle class." (for an alternative view, see Enns, 2015).

In this book, the primary questions that we examine concern whether health has a corresponding effect, i.e., how health problems affect political engagement and whether this effect is reflected in political outcomes. Obviously, this is a gradual process (see Jensen and van Kersbergen, 2017, pp. 115–16). The first step is preference formation: to what extent do citizens with good and poor health have different attitudes, perceptions and policy preferences? The second is preference articulation: to what extent do citizens with good or poor health differ in terms of their resources and motivation to participate in political processes, and are there any variations between different modes of participation? The third step is preference aggregation: do political elites respond equally to input from citizens with different levels of health?

These questions are important, not only for groups suffering from health problems, but also for the entire political system. In an inclusive democracy, the first step should be accessible to all kinds of citizens, regardless of their resources (Young, 2000). This is particularly warranted, since, in public debate, withdrawal from politics is sometimes regarded as a matter of individual choice, not involuntary exclusion and marginalization. Emphasizing the role of motivational factors may lead to the 'responsibilization' of the individual. From this point of view, people suffering from health problems simply do not take part in politics because they do not want to or are too preoccupied with other things to care. Too much concentration on motivational aspects ignores the association between various kinds of economic and societal inequalities and participation. In other words, it only emphasizes the motivation component in Verba, Schlozman and Brady's well-known civic voluntarism model (1995), while disregarding the potential effect of health on resources and mobilization.

Interpreting health-related differences in political engagement among citizens with poor health, mainly as a consequence of an individual's own choice, may build a kind of an 'empathy wall' (Hochschild, 2016) between citizens with and without health problems. As a concept, an empathy wall can be described as "an obstacle to deep understanding of another person" and his/her circumstances, which might be different than ours (ibid., 5). In the worst case scenario, such an empathy wall could lead to the failure to actively seek means by which to facilitate political engagement among citizens with health or functional limitations. In such a situation, disability status or poor health risks appear as more of a personal challenge than a social issue and a problem of citizenship (cf. Prince, 2014, p. 114). Yet, political participation is essentially collective action; ensuring its accessibility is also the responsibility of society. Schur, Kruse and Blanck's (2013, p. 237) conclusion crystallizes the benefits of inclusive democracy: "Making full use of talents of people with disabilities would strengthen the economy, and ensuring that everyone's voice is heard would make democracy stronger and more vibrant."

Health: definition and trends

There are many ways to conceptualize health. According to McDowell (2006, p. 11), our current understanding of health has come a long way, from considering health merely in terms of human survival to a current emphasis on quality of life. In a comprehensive account of health measures, Bowling (2005) distinguishes between functional (dis)ability, broader health status, mental health, social health, subjective well-being and quality of life. The last two are also closely linked to the concept of life satisfaction. McDowell (2006) offers a similar categorization, which makes a distinction between physical and mental health, as well as a more general assessment of life quality.

This multitude of health dimensions is, however, not present in the literature concerning health and political participation. In studies of political participation, operationalizations of health have mostly been limited to indicators of self-rated health (SRH) and functional disability. SRH has been one of the most (if not *the* most) widely used, single-item indicator of health in sociological medicine since the 1950s (Jylhä, 2009, p. 307). It reliably predicts a number of various aspects of health and health-promoting behaviour (e.g., Fylkesnes and Forde, 1992).

The SRH measure is a survey item, which asks the respondent to evaluate his/her overall health status on either a four-point or a five-point scale. In some cases, the question is framed such that the respondent is asked to evaluate personal health in comparison with peers. According to Jylhä (2009), to produce this estimate of personal health in a survey setting, the individual performs a multi-stage evaluation, which includes several considerations of the relevant components of one's health, previous illnesses and projections of future health, bodily sensations of various symptoms and comparisons with other people, among others. Segovia et al. (1989) found SRH to essentially measure a combination of worrying over health, suffering from a chronic medical condition or disability and estimating physical conditions and energy levels. A more recent study by Mavaddat et al. (2011) confirmed that SRH captures a multitude of physical, mental and social factors, although its predictive power is strongest in relation to physical health. In other words, assessments of SRH most reliably measure a person's physical condition rather than mental health or social functioning. According to Mavaddat et al. (2011, p. 803), this is compatible with the extensive body of literature, which has found SRH to be closely associated with the 'ability to perform physical functions'.

Despite the strong linkage between SRH and physical functioning, social scientists have also paid much attention to functional (dis)ability as a factor influencing political behaviour and participation (e.g., Schur et al., 2002). This is well grounded. As Bowling (2005, p. 4) explains: "[T]here is, then, a clear distinction between functioning and general health status. Functioning is directly related to the ability to perform one's roles and participate in life. As such, functional status is just one component of health – it is a measure of the effects of disease." Functional ability is therefore seen as directly related to a person's ability to act socially and societally, instead of a more general sense of one's condition measured by SRH. In our case, we are particularly interested in how people can fulfil their roles as democratic political citizens, even if their lives are hampered by disabilities or long-standing illnesses.

In our theoretical framework, we will primarily consider health in relation to SRH and functional disability. In addition to providing comparability with previous research, using these two indicators is warranted for other reasons. Firstly, they are especially robust as measures of physical problems limiting accessibility and mobility, which are both essential aspects for participating in politics. Secondly, SRH has typically been seen as indicating a more instantaneously produced assessment of personal well-being, whereas disability indicators have been used to measure more enduring, perhaps lifelong, conditions (e.g., Eikemo et al., 2008). Thirdly, whereas 'disability' typically entails a clinically diagnosed medical condition, a person can 'feel ill' and be seriously affected by the sensation without a detected disease. SRH indicators are essentially developed to capture this dimension of the effects of health (Bowling, 2005, pp. 1–2).

The distinction between acute and chronic illness is also relevant in the context of political behaviour. An acute, short-term illness, such as a flu, is likely to keep a person from voting if he/she happens to catch it on election day (Urbatsch, 2017). With the possible exception of extreme cases of influenza epidemics, for example, short-term medical conditions are not particularly interesting from the perspective of political behaviour. They do not constitute a predictable pattern that can be meaningfully studied in the context of political participation. The literature on SRH, however, shows that a person's likelihood of suffering from acute medical conditions is well captured by self-assessments of personal health; if a person repeatedly suffers from short-term illnesses, SRH is highly likely to indicate this.

Instead of short-term disruption in well-being, which routinely and temporarily affects each of us, our analysis focuses on health problems that are more long-standing. As Murrow and Oglesby (1996) have argued, a chronic or long-standing illness typically requires more care and resources if the patient wishes to maintain a normal lifestyle. Like any other aspect of a person's lifestyle, patterns of political behaviour are also likely to become affected by an enduring or chronic condition. Additionally, it seems plausible that the timing of when such an illness develops during the human life cycle will also influence the way in which a person interacts with the surrounding society. Suggested by the life cycle theory (also referred to as the adult roles theory), early adulthood is the time when political participation patterns develop and an individual reaches maturity as a political citizen (see e.g., Highton and Wolfinger, 2001). Health problems which have been present from birth or developed early in life can become an important building block in a person's social identity, which in turn shapes political behaviour. To be more precise, just as social identities are often considered to develop during adolescence and early adulthood (see e.g., Flanagan and Sherrod, 1998, p. 448), health-related behaviours are also formed during this period (Brooks-Gunn and

Graber, 1999). Development of a chronic illness during this vulnerable point in life could therefore have a particularly profound effect on political participation through the development of social identity.

A permanent disability, a severe illness or a chronic condition which develops at a later point in life could have similarly fundamental, but different, effects. A dramatic worsening of a person's health status often means the inability to continue working, as well as possibly having a negative effect on his/her social life. Dropping out of work means removing oneself from a workplace community, which might have a strong demobilizing impact when it comes to political participation. When this occurs at a later point in life, developing a social identity and a sense of belonging to a health group might not happen as easily as it does for people who have experienced health problems early in life.

In Finland, which forms the context of this study, healthcare-related issues continue to be a salient matter in elections, one after another. There are several reasons for this. First, the population is rapidly ageing. The average life expectancy in 2015 was 81 years of age, but is estimated to rise to 87 years by 2050, while the share of citizens over 65 years of age was 19 per cent in 2015 (27 per cent in 2050) (Health 2050, Demos Helsinki). With this changing population structure, maintaining a sustainable dependency ratio in the future is becoming an increasingly politicized question.

Second, differences in health and well-being are growing, even in universal welfare states, such as Finland (OECD, 2015). In spite of state-subsidized healthcare and social services, as well as the reimbursement of prescribed drugs, noteworthy discrepancies between various socio-economic groups in health and mortality have been reported (see e.g., Polvinen, 2016; Tarkiainen, 2016; Vaarama et al., 2014). Moreover, the association between income and mortality has grown stronger in Finland since the late 1980s (Tarkiainen, 2016). According to the National Institute for Health and Welfare (2014), health inequalities in Finland are explained mainly by differences in living and working conditions, as well as cultural and behavioural differences between various socio-economic groups. While such a social gradient in health is an uncontested fact, the ways to reduce and prevent health inequality, as well as ensure access to adequate healthcare for all citizens, remain hotly debated issues.

As shown in Table 1.1, the majority of respondents rate their health as good or better. As is always the case with survey data, the self-selection of respondents is a noteworthy factor in this respect. Those who suffer from ill health have a lower propensity to be recruited as survey respondents. This may be due to difficulties in targeting, especially if a person is currently staying in hospital or another institution, or has lower levels of motivation to participate because of illness. Hence, the differences in health are inevitably somewhat milder than in reality. The same applies to our other measure of health status concerning daily activities hampered by health problems (see Table 1.2).

Defining political engagement

We use the broad concept of political engagement to capture two important aspects in terms of an individual's relationship with politics: (1) participation in politics,

Table 1.1 Responses to the question, 'How is your health in general?' (%) (N = 1,995)

	%
Very good	25
Good	43
Fair	26
Bad	4
Very bad	1
Total	**100**

Table 1.2 Responses to question, 'Are you hampered in your daily activities in any way by any long-standing illness, disability, infirmity or mental health problem?' (%) (N = 1,998)

	%
Yes, a lot	7
Yes, to some extent	22
No	71
Total	**100**

understood as concrete acts, such as voting and taking part in demonstrations; and (2) political orientations, understood as ideological identifications and the motivation to follow politics without necessarily participating in it. Our conceptualization of political engagement therefore measures both what people do and what they think in terms of politics.

What we here refer to as 'political orientations' covers several aspects of cognitive engagement (see Gabriel, 2012). Firstly, we look at the extent to which ordinary people make an effort to follow and understand politics. To a great extent, this involves a question of motivation, which in the realm of politics comes down to the expression of an interest in politics (e.g., van Deth, 1990, pp. 276–7; Shani, 2009, p. 2). We also include political sophistication in order to see how health relates to the ability to grasp politics. Although political sophistication is often measured in terms of political knowledge or a sense of political efficacy, its theoretical roots are in ideologically constrained thinking, that is, the ability to understand politics through a robust ideological framework (Converse, 1964; Rapeli, 2013). Our conceptualization of political orientations therefore includes political interest, left-right self-identification and political knowledge.

The literature on the meaning of the other aspect of political engagement, political participation, is extensive. Teorell et al. (2007) proposed four conditions to define political participation: (1) action undertaken by individuals, (2) who are ordinary citizens, (3) with the intention to influence decisions taken by others (not everyday discussions and political interest) and (4) related to any political outcome in society (not only decisions made by public representatives and offi-cials). Political participation is also generally seen as clustering together vari-ous modes of participation. While voting is the fundamental form of political participation in a representative democracy, there is also a wide array of other activities. In their classic account, Verba and Nie (1972) recognized four forms of conventional political participation: voting, campaign activity, communal activity and contacting public officials. Barnes et al. (1979) also conceptualized uncon-ventional participation as including petition signings, demonstrations, boycotts, occupations, blockades, rent strikes and unofficial strikes (ibid., pp. 65–81). For them, conventional participation was also a broader concept, which consisted of reading about politics in newspapers, discussing politics with friends, working on community problems, contacting politicians or public officials, convincing friends to vote as self, participating in election campaigns and attending political meet-ings (ibid., pp. 84–7).

In a more recent account, Teorell et al. (2007) present a typology with five modes: voting, party activity (e.g., being a member of a party), consumer partici-pation (e.g., signing petitions and boycotting), protest activity (e.g., taking part in demonstrations and strikes) and contacting (e.g., politicians and civil servants). They base their typology on three criteria: channel of expression (representational or extra-representational), mechanism of influence (exit-based or voice-based) and scope (targeted or non-targeted towards specific democratic institutions).

Political participation therefore consists of various modes which ordinary citizens use to achieve a variety of political goals. In addition to the typologies presented above, from the perspective of health, there are also other possible approaches. Firstly, different forms of participation pose various practical obsta-cles to people with health problems. For instance, without proxy or hospital vot-ing or other facilitation mechanisms, the simple act of voting may be practically impossible for those with health problems. Secondly, it could be that people with health problems do not consider voting as the most effective means of making a difference. Those who wish to influence public health policy and protect the inter-ests of people with health problems are likely to choose other modes of participa-tion, which involve more direct access to decision making, such as contacts with politicians or authorities, party work or organizational activities. In the health framework, political participation can therefore be understood in terms of *acces-sibility* and *effectiveness*. Accessibility refers to physical obstacles which need to be overcome due to health problems, while effectiveness is concerned with the potential impact of each mode of participation.

The Finnish context

Besides the cross-national comparison in Chapter 6, our analysis is based on a survey conducted in Finland (see next section for details). A case study always raises the inevitable question of generalizability. As such, what does it mean to study health and political engagement in the Finnish context?

The overarching context in terms of the health–political engagement relation-ship is the Scandinavian welfare state model, which still seems to be the most suitable description of Finnish society. While no universally accepted definition of the welfare state exists, it has usually been used in a narrow sense in reference to "the various post-war state measures for the provision of key welfare services and social transfers. The welfare state is thereby used as a shorthand for the state's role in education, health, housing, poor relief, social insurance, in developed capitalist countries during the post-war period" (Eikemo and Bambra, 2008, p. 3).

In Finland, the role of the state in providing these services and arranging the redistribution of income has been quite extensive over a period of several decades. In terms of the healthcare system, Böhm et al. (2013, p. 263) have recently evaluated Finland as one of eight countries of the Organisation for Economic Co-operation and Development (OECD) with a 'national health service', as in a type of healthcare system where the public sector is mainly responsible for regulating and providing healthcare services for citizens. Along with the Nordic countries, Böhm et al. also include Portugal, Spain and the UK in this category.

While this is compelling evidence for the claim that Finland is the stereotypical Nordic welfare state, a word of caution is nevertheless in order. Updating the Esping-Andersen decommodification and stratification scores to identify liberal, conservative and social democratic 'ideal types', Ferragina and Seeleib-Kaiser (2011, p. 586; see also Esping-Andersen, 1990) do not identify Finland as one of the most socially democratic countries alongside Sweden, Norway and Denmark; instead, they locate Finland in the next, less socially democratic, category with the Netherlands. This is likely in reference to the various welfare cuts that have occurred in Finland since the deep economic recession of the early 1990s (Kettunen, 2001), which transformed Finland into a nation that was somewhat less 'Scandinavian' in terms of the reach of the welfare state model. All things considered, the analysis of health and citizens' political engagement in Finland should be understood against the backdrop of extensive public sector involvement in healthcare and other welfare-related services.

There are a few notable aspects in the Finnish political landscape. Firstly, Finland has a proportional electoral system with many national parties of significance. Currently, there are eight parties in the Finnish parliament. From the viewpoint of the individual citizen, there is plenty to choose from, but also many actors to monitor. An understandable consequence is that, although rates of political interest among the public are high, many find Finnish politics hard to grasp (Rapeli and Borg, 2016).

On the other hand, while the party system is fragmented, it is relatively stable (Karvonen, 2014). From all accounts, the political system, on the whole, should be considered as being rather predictable, while enjoying high legitimacy among citizens. Despite this stability, there has been plenty of concern about a declining electoral turnout, which has been more pronounced in Finland over the past few decades than in most other European democracies (Karvonen, 2014, p. 109). Other conventional forms of participation, such as party memberships, have also seen a steep decline.

From a comparative perspective, the view of political engagement in Finland is by no means depressing. In terms of both the more unconventional forms of participation, such as wearing badges and signing petitions, and the indicators of social capital and political trust, Finland scores relatively high on all counts (Bäck, 2011, pp. 84–108). Although turnout may be declining, Finnish citizens are politically interested, active and trusting of one another.

Regarding political trust, in particular, Finland is again a close companion of other Nordic countries (Grönlund and Setälä, 2007). As far as generalizability is concerned, this will obviously be most plausible in relation to the other Nordic countries and those continental European countries with similar welfare state profiles and patterns of citizen political engagement. For those countries that do not share these same characteristics, our study serves better as a point of comparison, rather than a source for drawing generalizable conclusions. Although any case study is necessarily more representative of some scenarios than others, we nevertheless do not see any reason to consider Finland as highly exceptional in any sense when it comes to an analysis of how health and political engagement interact.

Data

When trying to analyze the health–participation relationship, a typical problem is that it is nearly impossible to find data, which would include wide-ranging and reliable measures of both health and political engagement. For the purposes of this book, we gathered a new survey data set from Finland (see the Appendix for a more thorough description of all the data sets used in this book). In the survey, 2,001 respondents were asked questions on an extensive variety of aspects relating to health and engagement. For example, we included several items that measure individuals' general health and specific types of possible health problems they may have. However, as mentioned earlier, for the sake of brevity and comparability, we only use SRH and the disability measure in our analyses.

The problem with surveys in general is that, over the years, people have become increasingly reluctant to take part in them, a situation that may lead to serious biases in the analysis. It is extremely difficult to correct for this type of bias, but we have tried to do our best to ensure that the bias problems in our data are as small as possible. We have made linkages with several official data registers collected by Statistics Finland to collect more information on our target sample, using these data in connection with the information on who answered and who did not answer our survey. Then we used this information to derive weights to correct for biases produced by the survey collection process (see the Appendix for more details). Every survey data set suffers from biases, but we trust that these procedures will have considerably diminished the biases in our data.

We use the survey from Finland in Chapters 3 to 5. The cross-national comparison in Chapter 6 is based on the seven rounds of the European Social Survey and the sixth wave (2010–2014) of the World Values Survey. These data sets are also presented in more detail in the Appendix. Chapter 7 combines five health-related attitude measures from the Finnish survey data with the Voting Advice Application for the 2015 Finnish parliamentary elections made by the national broadcasting company YLE. To examine political representation, Chapter 7 compares responses to identical questions from the general public in our survey data with those from election candidates and elected MPs. This data set is also described in more detail in the Appendix.

Plan of the book

We continue the book by presenting our theoretical framework and hypotheses for the individual-level analyses of the relationship between health and political engagement in the next chapter. After testing these hypotheses, Chapters 3 to 5 deal with various aspects of this relationship, namely, health and different forms of political participation, health, political interest and efficacy and the impact of the social environment. Chapter 6 applies the individual-level analysis to a cross-national comparative perspective by assessing the impact of contextual factors, such as the electoral system, on the linkage between health and the four measures of political participation. Chapter 7 takes a different approach by looking at the political representation of different health groups on health-related issues. Instead of examining the impact of health on citizens' political engagement, the chapter examines the impact of health on getting one's voice heard in a democratic society. Finally, Chapter 8 summarizes the findings from each chapter and discusses the consequences for democratic politics, particularly from the viewpoint of political inequality.

References

Atkinson, A.B., 2015. *Inequality: What can be done?* Cambridge, MA: Harvard University Press.

Bäck, M., 2011. Socialt kapital och politiskt deltagande i Europa (in Swedish: Social capital and political participation in Europe). PhD. Åbo Akademi University.

Barnes, S. H., Max, K. and Allerbeck, K. L., 1979. *Political action: Mass participation in five Western democracies.* Beverly Hills, CA: Sage.

Blank, R.H. and Hines, Jr., S.M., 2001. *Biology and political science.* New York: Routledge.

Böhm, K., Schmid, A., Götze, R., Landwehr, C. and Rothgang, H., 2013. Five types of OECD healthcare systems: Empirical results of a deductive classification. *Health Policy*, 113(3), pp. 258–69.

Bowling, A., 2005. *Measuring health: A review of quality of life measurement scales.* Maidenhead: Open University Press.

Brooks-Gunn, J. and Graber, J.A., 1999. What's sex got to do with it? The development of health and sexual identities during adolescence. In R.J. Contrada and R.D. Ashmore, eds. *Self, social identity, and physical health: Interdisciplinary explorations.* New York: Oxford University Press, pp. 155–82.

Carpenter, D., 2012. Is health politics different? *Annual Review of Political Science*, 15, pp. 287–311.

Converse, P., 1964. The nature of belief systems in mass publics. In D. Apter, ed. *Ideology and discontent.* New York: Free Press, pp. 206–61.

Dorling, D., 2014. *Inequality and the 1%.* London: Verso Books.

Dorling, D., 2015, revised edition. *Injustice: Why social inequality still persists.* Bristol: Policy Press.

Eikemo, T. and Bambra, C., 2008. The welfare state: A glossary for public health. *Journal of Epidemiology and Community Health*, 62(1), pp. 3–6.

Eikemo, T., Huisman, M., Bambra, C. and Kunst, A., 2008. Health inequalities according to educational level in different welfare regimes: A comparison of 23 European countries. *Sociology of Health and Illness*, 30(4), pp. 565–82.

Enns, P.K., 2015. Relative policy support and coincidental representation. *Perspectives on Politics*, 13(4), pp. 1053–64.

Esping-Andersen, G., 1990. *The three worlds of welfare capitalism*. Padstow: Polity Press.

Ferragina, E. and Seeleib-Kaiser, M., 2011. Welfare regime debate: Past, present, futures? *Policy and Politics*, 39(4), pp. 583–611.

Flanagan, C.A. and Sherrod, L., 1998. Youth political development: An introduction. *Journal of Social Issues*, 54(3), pp. 447–56.

Fylkesnes, K. and Forde, O.H., 1992. Determinants and dimensions involved in self-evaluation of health. *Social Science and Medicine*, 35(3), pp. 271–9.

Gabriel, O., 2012. Cognitive political engagement. In S.I. Keil and O.W. Gabriel, eds. *Society and democracy in Europe*. Abingdon: Routledge, pp. 162–84.

Galbraith, J.K., 2016. *Inequality: What everyone needs to know*. Oxford: Oxford University Press.

Gilens, M., 2015. The insufficiency of "democracy by coincidence": A response to Peter K. Enns. *Perspectives on Politics*, 13(4), 1065–71.

Grönlund, G. and Wass, H. eds., 2016. Poliittisen osallistumisen eriytyminen: Eduskuntavaalitutkimus 2015 (in Finnish: The differentiation of political participation – the Finnish National Election Study 2015). Helsinki: Ministry of Justice.

Grönlund, K. and Setälä, M., 2007. Political trust, satisfaction and voter turnout. *Comparative European Politics*, 5(4), pp. 400–22.

Grusky, D.B. and Kricheli-Katz, T. eds., 2012. *The new gilded age: The critical inequality debates of our time*. Stanford, CA: Stanford University Press.

Highton, B. and Wolfinger, R.E., 2001. The first seven years of the political life cycle. *American Journal of Political Science*, 45(1), pp. 202–9.

Hiilamo, H. and Kangas, O., 2014. Cherry picking: How sensitive is the relationship between inequality and social problems to country samples. *International Journal of Sociology and Social Policy*, 34(11/12), pp. 771–92.

Hochschild, A.R., 2016. *Strangers in their own land: Anger and mourning on the American right*. New York: The New Press.

Jensen, C. and van Kersbergen, K., 2017. *The politics of inequality*. London: Palgrave Macmillan.

Jylhä, M., 2009. What is self-rated health and why does it predict mortality? Towards a unified conceptual model. *Social Science and Medicine*, 69(3), pp. 307–16.

Karvonen, L., 2014. *Parties, governments and voters in Finland*. Colchester: ECPR Press.

Kettunen, P., 2001. The Nordic welfare state in Finland. *Scandinavian Journal of History*, 26(3), pp. 225–47.

Marmot, M., 2015. *The health gap: The challenge of an unequal world*. London: Bloomsbury.

Mavaddat, N., Kinmonth, A.L., Sanderson, S., Surtees, P., Bingham, S. and Shaw, K.T., 2011. What determines self-rated health (SRH)? A cross-sectional study of SF-36 health domains in the EPIC-Norfolk cohort. *Journal of Epidemiology and Community Health*, 65(9), pp. 800–6.

McDowell, I., 2006. *Measuring health: A guide to rating scales and questionnaires*. New York: Oxford University Press.

Murrow, E. and Oglesby, M., 1996. Acute and chronic illness: Similarities, differences and challenges. *Orthopedic Nursing*, 15(5), pp. 47–51.

The National Institute for Health and Welfare, 2014. *Health inequalities* [online] Available through: <www.thl.fi/en/web/health-and-welfare-inequalities/health-care-cervices> [Accessed 27 February 2017].

OECD, 2015. *Health at glance*. Paris: OECD Publishing.

Peterson, Steven A., 1990. *Political behavior: patterns in everyday life*. Newbury Park: Sage.

Pickett, K.E. and Wilkinson, R.G., 2015. Income inequality and health: A causal review. *Social Science and Medicine*, 128(2015), pp. 316–26.

Polvinen, A., 2016. *Socioeconomic status and disability retirement in Finland: Causes, changes over time and mortality*. Helsinki: Finnish Centre for Pensions.

Prince, M.J., 2014. Enabling the voter participation of Canadians with disabilities, reforming Canada's electoral systems. *Canadian Journal of Disability Studies*, 3(2), 95–120.

Putnam, R.E., 2015. *Our kids: The American dream in crisis*. New York: Simon & Schuster.

Rapeli, L., 2013. *The conception of citizen knowledge in democratic theory*. Basingstoke: Palgrave Macmillan.

Rapeli, L. and Borg, S., 2016. Kiinnostavaa, mutta monimutkaista: tiedot, osallistuminen ja suhtautuminen vaikuttamiseen (in Finnish: Interesting, but complicated: Knowledge, participation and attitudes toward influencing politics). In K. Grönlund and H. Wass, eds. *Poliittisen osallistumisen eriytyminen: Eduskuntavaalitutkimus 2015* (in Finnish: *The differentiation of political participation – the Finnish National Election Study 2015*). Helsinki: Ministry of Justice, pp. 358–78.

Savage, M., 2015. *Social class in the 21th century*. London: Penguin Books.

Schur, L., Kruse, D. and Blanck, P., 2013. *People with disabilities, sidelined or mainstreamed?* Cambridge: Cambridge University Press.

Schur, L., Shields, T., Kruse, D. and Schriner, K., 2002. Enabling democracy: Disability and voter turnout. *Political Research Quarterly*, 55(1), pp. 167–90.

Segovia, J., Bartlett, R. and Edwards, A.C., 1989. An empirical analysis of the dimensions of health status measures. *Social Science and Medicine*, 29(6), pp. 761–8.

Shani, D., 2009. *On the origins of political interest*. PhD. Princeton University.

Smets, K. and van Ham, C., 2013. The embarrassment of riches? A meta-analysis of individual-level research on voter turnout. *Electoral Studies*, 32(2), pp. 344–59.

Stiglitz, J.E., 2012. *The price of inequality: How today's divided society endangers our future*. New York: W.W. Norton & Company.

Tarkiainen, L., 2016. *Income and mortality – the dynamics of disparity: A study on the changing association between income and mortality in Finland*. Helsinki: University of Helsinki.

Teorell, J., Torcal, M. and Montero, J.R., 2007. Political participation: Mapping the terrain. In J.W. van Deth, J.R. Montero and A. Westholm, eds. *Citizenship and involvement in European democracies: A comparative analysis*. London: Routledge, pp. 334–57.

Therborn, G., 2013. *The killing fields of inequality*. Cambridge: Polity Press.

Urbatsch, R., 2017. Influenza and voter turnout. *Scandinavian Political Studies*, 40(1), pp. 107–19.

Vaarama, M., Karvonen, S., Kestilä, L., Moisio, P. and Muuri, A., 2014. *Suomalaisen hyvinvointi* (in Finnish: *Well-being in Finland*). Helsinki: National Institute for Health and Welfare.

Van Deth, J.W., 1990. Interest in politics. In M.K. Jennings and J.W. van Deth, eds. *Continuities in political action*. New York: De Gruyter, pp. 275–312.

Verba, S. and Nie, N.H., 1972. *Participation in America: Political democracy and social equality*. New York: Harper and Row.

Verba, S., Schlozman, K.L. and Brady, H.E., 1995. *Voice and equality: Civic voluntarism in American politics*. Cambridge, MA: Harvard University Press.

Wilkinson, R., and Pickett, K., 2009. *The spirit level: Why more equal societies almost always do better*. London: Allen Lane.

Wilkinson, R. and Pickett, K., 2010. *The spirit level: Why equality is better for everyone*. London: Penguin Books.

Young, I.M., 2000. *Inclusion and democracy*. Oxford: Oxford University Press.

2   Theoretical framework

We begin this chapter with an extensive review of previous research to establish where the discipline currently stands. We then present our theoretical framework and hypotheses, which build on existing theories of political engagement. The hypotheses will then be tested in the following three chapters.

Previous research

Although the relationship between health and political engagement has not been one of the primary targets of mainstream research in the broader study of political behaviour, an impressive and growing number of studies has nevertheless addressed the issue. Our conceptualization of political engagement, as explained in Chapter 1, does not include the broad notion of social capital. This leads us to disregard the extensive body of literature on the linkage between health and social capital, which tends to conclude that poor social capital is linked to poor health (e.g., Macinko and Starfield, 2001; Almedom, 2005; Islam et al., 2006). The literature, which we focus on, is a mixed set of studies on both individual and aggregate levels, including several combinations of various health and engagement variables. Tables 2.1 and 2.2 present an overview of this literature in terms of the level of analysis and key variables. The overview does not claim to be an exhaustive catalogue of everything published on the topic. Rather, it wishes to provide a realistic and useful summary, which is representative of the entire body of literature.

Table 2.1 reports individual-level studies, while Table 2.2 reports aggregate-level studies. As the tables suggest, the literature can be divided according to both the health and the political engagement measures used in the analyses. Regarding health, a division between (1) those analyzing personal health and (2) those analyzing disability can be made. Personal health is usually measured in terms of the status of self-rated health (SRH), whereas disability typically refers to a physical impairment. In terms of political engagement, the studies rely on three types of indicators, which are effectively identical with our operationalization: (1) voting, (2) other forms of participation, and (3) political orientations (which include left-right ideology, partisanship and political efficacy). These are typical indicators of what is often referred to as cognitive political engagement, i.e., the extent to

Table 2.1 Individual-level studies: type of health and political engagement indicators and dependent variables

PERSONAL HEALTH		DISABILITY	
Political participation	*Ideology*	*Political participation*	*Ideology*
Dependent variable: health	*Dependent variable: health*	*Dependent variable: voting*	*Dependent variable: ideology*
Brody and Sniderman (1977)	Cockerham et al. (2006)	Schur and Kruse (2000)	Gastil (2000)
Blakely et al. (2001)	Subramanian et al. (2009)	Karp and Banducci (2001)	Schur and Adya (2012)
Hyyppä and Mäki (2003)	Huijts et al. (2010)	Schur et al. (2002)	
Chan and Chiu (2007)	Subramanian et al. (2010)	Schur et al. (2005b)	
Sundquist and Yang (2007)	Subramanian and Perkins (2010)	Schur and Adya (2012)	
Arah (2008)		Schur et al. (2013)	
Bryngelsson (2009)		Matsubayashi and Ueda (2014)	
d'Hombres et al. (2010)		Miller and Powell (2016)	
Gustafsson et al. (2013)			
Dependent variable: voting		*Dependent variable: other form(s) of participation*	
Bazargan et al. (1991)			
Bukov et al. (2002)		Gastil (2000)	
Goerres (2006)		Schur et al. (2003)	
Denny and Doyle (2007a)		Schur et al. (2005a)	
Denny and Doyle (2007b)		Mattila and Papageorgiou (2016)	
Denny and Doyle (2009)			
Bhatti and Hansen (2012)			
Mattila et al. (2013)			
Nygård and Jakobsson (2013)			
Gollust and Rahn (2015)			
Pacheco and Fletcher (2015)			
Hassell and Settle (2017)			
Lahtinen et al. (2017)			
Sund et al. (2017)			
Wass et al. (2017)			

PERSONAL HEALTH	
Political participation	*Ideology*

Dependent variable: other form(s) of participation

Peterson (1987)

Peterson (1990)

Ojeda (2015)

Söderlund and Rapeli (2015)

Burden et al. (2017)

Table 2.2 Aggregate-level studies: type of health and political engagement indicators and dependent variables

PERSONAL HEALTH

POLITICAL PARTICIPATION

Dependent variable: health

Davey Smith and Dorling (1996)
Kondrichin and Lester (1998)
Kawachi et al. (1999)
Kondrichin and Lester (1999)
Dorling et al. (2001)
Kelleher et al. (2002)
Navarro et al. (2003)
Cummins et al. (2005)
Navarro et al. (2006)
Mackenbach and McKee (2013)
Shin and McCarthy (2013)

Dependent variable: voting

Gleason (2001)
Page et al. (2002)
Shaw et al. (2002)
Reitan (2003)
Urbatsch (2017)

which a person is psychologically attached to politics and has the ability to understand it (e.g., Gabriel, 2012). Another important distinction concerns the dependent variable. While most studies, especially those by political scientists, employ political engagement as the dependent variable, in health-related disciplines the assumed direction of causality is reversed. We therefore distinguish the different studies based on the dependent variable.

A comparison of the tables shows that research has concentrated more on individual-level than aggregate-level analysis, as well as slightly more on personal health than disability. As far as political engagement is concerned, there is a heavy emphasis on voting. The number of studies examining other forms of participation or some form of cognitive attachment to politics is significantly lower.

Previous research has treated both health/disability and some form of political engagement as the dependent variable. Scholars have, in other words, seen health as both a cause and a consequence of political engagement. For political scientists, political engagement has been a more obvious choice for a dependent variable. They typically see health disparities as a potential source of variation in patterns of political behaviour. Scholars from fields such as social medicine, on the other hand, also consider variations in health as a consequence of political engagement.

Health and political participation

Most studies falling into this category have used voting as the dependent variable and included personal health as one of several independent variables. Some have switched this design around and instead modelled voting as a determinant of health. In these analyses, voting is considered an indicator of social connectedness or social capital, which is found to be associated with variations in personal health. For example, Sundquist and Yang (2007), when investigating Swedish data, found that higher rates of social capital, measured as turnout in a neighbourhood, were related to better personal health. Blakely et al. (2001) present similar results from the US. They found that variation in turnout among socio-demographic groups explains differences in personal health, including when taking into account individual- and state-level differences in income. Arah (2008) draws similar conclusions in an analysis from the UK.

While most of these analyses employ SRH as the health indicator, some do not. Bryngelsson (2009), for instance, uses sick leave absences as an indicator of health and finds no statistically significant association between health and voting in Sweden, suggesting that non-voting ought not to be uncritically accepted as an indicator of social exclusion, as much of the comparable literature does. Meanwhile, Gustafsson et al. (2013), who also studied the situation in Sweden by using disability pension as the dependent variable, found that social isolation and low political participation predicted living on a disability pension. Although inconclusive, the results suggest that voting is a determinant of a person's degree of social connectedness. Whether voting should be used as a proxy for social capital is, however, debatable.

Turning the variables the other way around, poor health also seems to decrease the likelihood of turning out to vote. The magnitude of the effect varies between approximately 4 percentage points in the UK (Denny and Doyle, 2007b) and up to 12 in the US (Pacheco and Fletcher, 2015), while a comparative study by Mattila et al. (2013) and an analysis by Denny and Doyle from Ireland (2007a) estimate the effect between these extremes. According to Pacheco and Fletcher (2015, p. 109), the impact of poor health on voting was found to rival that of other key predictors, such as parents' education, race and marital status. The findings therefore strongly support the idea of including health in models estimating voting propensity.

This literature typically relies on the SRH measure, which is a useful indicator, although it fails to distinguish between different types of health problems, which could relate differently to political engagement. A growing number of studies has recently addressed the issue by using more versatile measures of health. For instance, Gollust and Rahn (2015) show that people with cancer are more likely to vote compared with people with heart disease. Additionally, African Americans and people with limited education, who also suffer from cancer, are particularly active voters. The impact of poor health on voting is therefore not a universally depressing one. Instead, Gollust and Rahn suggest that it depends primarily on two factors: mobilization and self-interest. People with cancer are well organized through patient associations, which could have a significant mobilizing effect on this particular group of people, while suffering from a health problem.

Ojeda (2015) has focused on depression, finding a negative connection with both voting and other types of participation. In a similar fashion to Gollust and Rahn (2015), Sund et al. (2017) also find that cancer increases voting propensity. Using register-based data, Sund et al. further discovered that neurodegenerative brain diseases, such as dementia, as well as alcoholism and depression, have particularly strong negative associations with voting. Burden et al. (2017) provide more evidence, showing that distinguishing between various types of health problems could reveal different patterns of political behaviour. According to the analysis of US register data, cognitive malfunctioning is detrimental to any kind of political participation, while physical limitations are especially significant obstacles for voting. In another recent study, Hassell and Settle (2016) show that the effect of stress on voting propensity is contingent on previous voting habits: stress experiences only lower voting propensity among people who did not have a habit of voting from the time before the presentation of stress. The finding therefore suggests that patterns of political behaviour are affected differently by declining health, depending on what those patterns were before health started having an impact on political engagement.

The scholarly scope is, however, still rather narrow in terms of how political engagement is measured. There is a very strong focus on voting, although, for example, Burden et al. (2017) and Ojeda (2015) have recently broadened the scope somewhat. The most recent study devoted to participation, besides voting, by Söderlund and Rapeli (2015), found that in Scandinavian countries, poor health increases the likelihood of wearing a campaign badge or sticker, contacting a politician or public official and taking part in a lawful demonstration. The relationship between health and political participation is thus by no means a one-way street where health problems inevitably lead to less activity. Whether health problems lead to more or less participation depends on the nature of the health problem, as well as on the chosen form of participation.

Health and ideology

A handful of studies has looked at how political ideology relates to health. These studies consider health as the outcome variable and ideology as a possible explanatory variable, thus suggesting that a person's political identity leads to differences in personal health. Cockerham et al. (2006) look at Belarus, Russia and Ukraine and find that people with pro-communist beliefs lead unhealthier lives. A self-proclaimed rightist ideology on the left-right (or liberal-conservative) continuum is found to predict better health than leftist ideology in the US, Europe and Japan (Huijts, Subramanian and Perkins, 2010; Subramanian et al., 2010; Subramanian, Huijts and Perkins, 2009; Subramanian and Perkins, 2010).

According to Subramanian et al. (2010, p. 838), the available evidence shows that the relationship is not only a manifestation of differences in socio-economic status, but related to differences in values towards religion and societal roles, for example. It therefore seems likely that the relationship between political ideology and health could be indicative of something much beyond pure political preferences, such as outlook on life in general. But there is an obvious need for a better understanding of the direction of the causal chain between health and ideology; do political convictions change when health status changes or does health status always precede the formation of political self-identification? The existing literature is essentially silent on this matter.

Disability and political participation

Turning to disability, we find again an emphasis on voting, although some studies have also looked at the impact of disability on other forms of political participation. The studies by Gastil (2000) and Schur and Adya (2012) are, to our knowledge, the only ones that have looked at the relationship between disability and (party) ideology. Looking at the US, Schur and Adya (2012) find that identifying with the Democratic Party is more common among people with a disability compared with the entire population.

The disability literature has focused particularly on analyzing how disability hinders political participation and if, for example, voting facilitation mechanisms manage to lower the costs of voting for people with disabilities. Concentrating on voting seems warranted, given that disability diminishes turnout by 10 percentage points (Schur and Kruse, 2000). Measures aimed at making voting more convenient are, however, not very effective in closing this gap in turnout; instead, they may further activate groups that are already voting in large numbers (Karp and Banducci, 2001; Matsubayashi and Ueda, 2014). Miller and Powell (2016) offer a glimpse of optimism by showing that the opportunity to cast a vote by mail is helpful for the disabled.

In addition to a sizable turnout gap, Schur et al. (2003) also report lower levels of efficacy. The rather pessimistic picture of political engagement, which is almost exclusively based on US data, is made slightly less bleak by Schur et al. (2005a), who find that, among young people with disability, participation levels are equal to those among non-disabled peers. Moreover, Mattila and Papageorgiou (2016) show that, although there is a turnout gap, the disabled are more active than the non-disabled in demonstrations and direct contacts with politicians.

Aggregate-level studies

A smaller, but highly relevant, body of literature has examined connections between various health indicators, such as mortality, SRH and obesity, and political participation, almost exclusively measured as voting, on the aggregate level. The research objective in the literature is to see whether various contexts, such as neighbourhoods in cities, states or entire countries, can be associated with differences in the health–engagement linkage. In particular, researchers within the health sciences, such as social medicine, have tended to use political participation as an explanation for different health outcomes, while social scientists have typically reversed this causal chain. The studies do not, however, explicitly assume causality, but speak in a more relaxed manner of 'associations'. This suggests that the direction of causality is again debatable and that scholars tend to see societal circumstances and community health as a reciprocal relationship.

Several studies from the British Isles have shown that, both in the UK and in Ireland, mortality rates are higher in areas with left-wing party dominance (Davey Smith and Dorling, 1996; Dorling et al., 2001; Kelleher et al., 2002; Cummins et al., 2005). The UK, with a relatively clear-cut difference between two large parties representing the political left and the right, as well as corresponding living areas, seems to have attracted many scholars to look for aggregate-level associations. To a lesser degree, scholars have also turned to the US, which provides a similar partisan context. Shin and McCarthy (2013) find a positive relationship between obesity and the Republican vote at the county level, suggesting that health behaviours and political choices are connected. Kawachi et al. (1999) make a more general discovery by finding that, in US states with lower rates of political participation, mortality rates are also higher.

A few studies offer a broader perspective by showing that the ideology of the government affects health outcomes in a country. While MacKenbach and McKee (2013) are more cautious about reporting a positive association between social democratic regimes and positive health status among citizens, Navarro et al. (2006) find stronger evidence suggesting that egalitarian policies lead to positive health outcomes. Indicative of the reciprocity of community health and political participation, Page et al. (2002) also find a strong positive connection between right-wing governance and suicide rates, although they employed voting as the dependent variable. Regardless of how the causality is conceived, community health seems poorer under right-wing political rule, at least in the British context. Using US data, Urbatsch (2017) makes a useful contribution to the literature by showing that influenza, which is not a permanent health problem, also negatively affects turnout. The finding implies that random epidemics may also have political consequences, which are quite impossible to anticipate or control.

The current state of research

The individual-level link between SRH and voting has been the most heavily studied subject in the literature so far, while the link between disability and voting has also received a lot of attention. Other forms of political participation are slowly, but surely, receiving more scholarly interest, although cognitive engagement (political interest, ideological thinking, sense of efficacy) has received much less consideration from academics in the field. How health relates to these fundamental drivers of political behaviour is still, to a large extent, unknown. Although the disability literature has done well in documenting the gap in turnout, which puts the disabled at a representational disadvantage, the field is dominated by studies from the US context. The impact of egalitarian institutions and multiparty governance on the political engagement of disabled persons, for instance, therefore remains largely unidentified.

As already noted, another aspect that our overview identified as requiring more work concerns the diversification of the operationalization of health. Although SRH and disability will undoubtedly remain useful indicators of health, a more nuanced treatment of health should be one of the focal points of future research, as Burden et al. (2017), in particular, have called for. The argument receives further support from the findings of Urbatsch (2017), which show that local outbreaks of common illnesses, such as influenza, during election time may have serious political implications.

The most obvious need for improvement concerns cross-national and aggregate-level analyses. While the arrow of causality has yet to be established between community health and political engagement, we also know very little about how the ideology of democratic regimes and other system-level factors affect the individual-level relationship between health and political engagement. Considering the huge variation in, for example, the extent of redistributive policies in different countries, there is reason to believe that health and engagement have rather different relationships depending on the political context. The lack of a better understanding of the role of political institutions and context is partly due to deficiencies in the theoretical trajectories for explaining health and political engagement. There is surprisingly little discussion about the theoretical relationships, let alone the direction of assumed causality, in the literature. In the following section, we offer some pathways through which health and political engagement can plausibly be linked together in theoretical terms. While the following applies to the individual level, in Chapter 6 we extend our theoretical framework and empirical inquiry to cross-national comparisons as well.

A theoretical framework for connecting health and political engagement

Although personal health is not as such included in theories explaining political engagement, there are many ways in which to incorporate it into existing frameworks. The empirical literature, as previously reviewed, typically uses resource theory or its close companion, the civic voluntarism model, to build a theoretical case for health and political engagement. We suggest that theories emphasizing social context and identity, as well as self-interest theory, also offer useful theoretical pathways for integrating health into models of political engagement.

Resource theory

Undoubtedly, the most widely used and perhaps the most intuitive model for approaching political participation through health is resource theory. Sometimes used interchangeably with the civic voluntarism model, the theory is based on factors that account for individual differences in political participation: ability, motivation and mobilization. In their famous quote, Verba et al. (1995, p. 269) summarize three fundamental reasons for not participating: "because people can't, they don't want to or nobody asked them". From this perspective, political passivity occurs when people "lack resources, because they lack psychological engagement with politics, or because they are outside of the recruitment networks that bring people into politics" (ibid.).

Thus, although resource theory can easily be mistaken for only emphasizing socio-economically determined resources, such as time, money and civic skills, it also extends to cognitive engagement and mobilization, which are seen as distinct forms of resources. The fundamental premise, nevertheless, is that resources and participation have a positive connection: having more resources lowers all types of hurdles for participation, thus leading to more political action. In this context, health can be seen as another type of resource that affects political activity. Generally speaking, resource theory expects poor health to decrease participation because it raises the costs of participation by imposing concrete obstacles and consumes time and energy, which are then deducted from what could have been spent on political engagement. This suggests a generic hypothesis according to which *poor health decreases political engagement* (H1).

It could, however, be argued that this assumption may only hold for people who started experiencing health problems after the crucial formative years of adolescence or early adulthood, given that their political behaviour patterns were formed when health problems did not yet diminish resources for political participation. Those who either were born with a limiting health condition or had it when their social identities were formed during early adulthood might not regard their health problem as a 'lack of resource', but as part of normal life instead. Therefore, even if health, undoubtedly in an objective sense, makes participation more difficult, people may respond differently to health-related obstacles, depending on how these relate to their personal health. The opposite seems plausible, too: if a health problem has been present since childhood, a habit of engaging in politics may not have been formed in the first place, whereas people who start experiencing health problems later in life may nevertheless continue participating in politics if they have developed such a habit. To examine these two alternative scenarios, we test a more specific hypothesis according to which *health decreases political engagement less among people who have experienced health problems, at least since childhood* (H2).

Self-interest theory

Whereas resource theory suggests that poor health will lead to relative political passivity, self-interest theory gives reason to expect that health problems may in fact spur people on towards more action by creating strong incentives for participation.

Much like the traditional rational choice approach, self-interest theory also maintains that, ultimately, human behaviour is driven by the attempt to maximize personal gain. As Sears and Funk note, in the field of politics, self-interest is likely to matter only in situations where individuals are highly motivated to pursue personal gain (1991, p. 58). When the expected payoff is low, compared with the required investment, self-interest does not seem to affect behaviour. Experiencing health problems, however, could potentially be a motivating factor, which causes people to act in pure self-interest; when personal health is at stake, the payoff for a favourable policy outcome is arguably unusually high, even when the costs of participation are high.

In similar fashion, conflict theory adds to the theoretical case by suggesting that poor health could be conducive to political engagement. It suggests that (perceived) inequality may instead increase people's engagement in politics because higher levels of inequality cause disagreements in political debates, fuelling competition between policy choices and mobilizing people into action (Solt, 2008). Furthermore, in this case, poor health ought to become a motivator because people suffering from health problems are often dependent on social benefits, meaning that they have a lot at stake in certain policy debates (see also Söderlund and Rapeli, 2015).

From a self-interest perspective, people with health problems could therefore be seen as a group with potentially very high benefits and high motivation: being more or less dependent on public health services, they have a genuine and unusually large economic incentive to vote for the optimal party or candidate. This approach suggests a hypothesis which stands in direct contrast with H1, namely, that *poor health increases political engagement* (H3). This hypothesis should, however, be seen as applying to people whose health, although poor, nevertheless allows them to participate in politics. When health problems become very serious, political engagement will certainly be negatively affected if a person is, for example, hospitalized. In such cases, however, people will also become unavailable as survey respondents, and consequently fall outside the empirical scope of typical analyses.

This generic assumption could be developed further to account for socioeconomic status, thus building a bridge between resource theory and self-interest theory. It could be theorized that poor health may only boost political engagement among people who find themselves in a vulnerable socio-economic position. People who do not depend on political decisions and the public sector for getting proper care for their health problems seem unlikely to become particularly motivated by health problems in order to be politically engaged. People who do rely on the public healthcare system, however, are arguably the ones whose potential benefits and motivation levels are high. Spending on public health services has historically been clearly linked to leftist parties. Consequently, *people with low socio-economic status and poor health are expected to have above-average rates of political engagement* (H4).

Theories of social context

Political engagement has also been explained through environmental or contextual factors, which affect how individuals engage with politics. Broadly speaking, two different approaches can be distinguished: the contextual model and the social identity model.

The contextual model of political behaviour argues that social environments affect the way people behave politically and consist of various social institutions, such as voluntary organizations, workplaces, educational institutions and religious communities, which together form the context in which a person makes political choices. According to the model, the character of a person's living environment affects those social behavioural patterns that people learn and adopt (Timpone, 1998; Beaudoin and Thorson, 2004; Baybeck and McClurg, 2005, pp. 494–65, for a review; see also McClurg, 2003). In a similar vein, the mobilization model also asserts that political participation is a function of opportunities and encouragement from other people. As with the social capital model (e.g., Putnam, 2000), this approach emphasizes the impact of a person's social connectedness and living environment as determinants of political behaviour patterns.

In terms of health and political engagement, this theoretical trajectory suggests that social environment could affect the association between health and political engagement. The impact of health on engagement could, therefore, depend on whether the social environment of the individual lowers hurdles for engagement or makes engagement even more laborious. We hypothesize that *social connections are more important determinants of political engagement among people with health problems than among people in good health* (H5). In other words, we assume that the extent to which poor health has a negative impact on engagement is contingent on a person's social environment: a well-functioning social network will have a mobilizing effect and be conducive to political engagement, while lacking such a boost will be particularly detrimental to people suffering from health problems, compared with their healthy counterparts.

Furthermore, the contextual model of political behaviour has an obvious overlap with the resource model, given that health affects political participation through mobilization. Meanwhile, social networks facilitate active participation and can make a big difference to people with health problems, who may need both practical assistance and encouragement from their community in order to become mobilized for action. A social environment can either encourage or discourage participation through a sense of belonging or by providing much needed practical

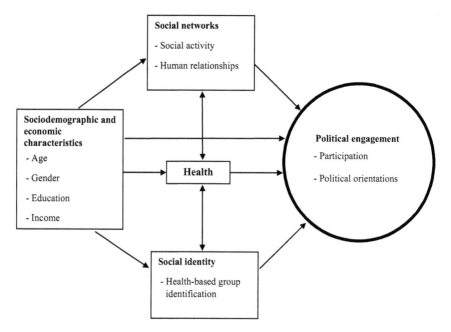

Figure 2.1 Resources and social context: a theoretical framework

help in order, for example, to turn out to vote or attend local meetings. People with health problems seem particularly likely to be affected by the nature of their community.

In addition to environments, the formation of our personal identities moulds political behaviour and engagement as well. Collective identity theory attempts to explain how shared identities spur people towards taking political action. A collective identity is the shared experience of a group originating from its members' common interests, experiences and solidarities (Whooley, 2007). Such an identity can be based on a number of different factors or conditions, which potentially define a person's status and relation to the surrounding world: ethnicity, gender, language, occupation, social class, etc.

In this case, we analyze the relevance of a health-based identity for political engagement. We could, for instance, expect strong, health-related social identities to develop when a sickness or disability has developed early in life or been present since birth. For people with a long-standing health issue, a strong sense of a social identity could develop, which is linked to the health problem, even if it develops later in life. This could lead to high-intensity activism involving, for example, voluntary organizations that seek benefits for people suffering from similar conditions or direct contacts with decision makers with the aim of affecting health policy. We therefore make two assumptions: firstly, we hypothesize that *identifying with others who experience health problems increases the propensity for political engagement among people with health problems* (H6);

Table 2.3 Hypotheses

Resource theory:

---

1. *Poor health decreases political engagement.*
2. *Poor health decreases political engagement to a lesser extent among people who have experienced health problems, at least since childhood.*

Self-interest theory:

---

3. *Poor health increases political engagement.*
4. *People with poor health and low socio-economic status have above-average rates of political engagement.*

Contextual theory:

---

5. *Social connections are more important determinants of political engagement among people with health problems than among people in good health.*

Social identity theory:

---

6. *Identifying with others who experience health problems increases the propensity for political engagement among people with health problems*
7. *Identifying with others who experience health problems increases the propensity for demanding forms of political engagement among people with health problems.*

---

secondly, we assume that *identifying with others who experience health problems increases the propensity for demanding forms of political engagement among people with health problems* (H7). Theoretically, our reasoning follows Melucci (1996, pp. 70–2), who sees collective identity as intimately linked to political action (see also Polletta and Jasper, 2001). Our hypotheses therefore presuppose that a sense of identifying with other people who also suffer from a health problem matters with regard to political engagement.

Empirical analysis of causality is notoriously complicated and our analyses in this book do not allow us to verify, in any strict sense, causal chains between health and political variables. Neither do we claim to do so. Nevertheless, we combine resource theory and the theories of social identities and social contexts to construct a tentative theoretical model, which implies possible causal linkages between health, political engagement and some intervening factors. The arrows in Figure 2.1 depict assumed causal linkages, although we are not prepared to make strong causality claims with our analysis. The model in Figure 2.1, although simplified, serves two purposes. Firstly, it clarifies how we think about the possible underlying mechanisms behind the variables that we analyze throughout the book; in turn, this provides us with a framework that guides our analysis in the subsequent chapters. Secondly, we hope the model will inspire future analyses, which will hopefully benefit from using data that are able to reveal those causalities that we can only currently theorize about.

Let us recap the hypotheses, which will guide the detailed analyses in Chapters 3 to 5 (Table 2.3).

Some of the limitations to the above framework should be noted. Firstly, our theoretical framework only considers health as a personal property, even though people can also be affected by the health problems of their family members, and even those of close friends. Consequently, an investigation into health and political engagement could also consider the above theories in light of close human relationships, not merely as a phenomenon that only concerns directly affected individuals themselves. Secondly, the framework does not make explicit assumptions about which dimensions of health are related to specific modes of engagement. Instead, it adopts a more general approach where the primary focus is on whether and how health problems contribute to the development of a person's political behaviour patterns. The framework therefore implicitly presupposes that health can be reliably measured through the most commonly used indicators measuring SRH and disability. More specific hypotheses regarding the connections between, for example, mental versus physical health and political participation are, of course, possible and desirable in the context of further research. Theories of political engagement do not, however, offer clear reasons as to why, for example, poor mental health, but not poor physical health, ought to lead to different patterns of political participation; here, it is simply assumed that, although the *mechanisms* may be different, the *outcome* of poor health for participation is the same, regardless of the nature of the health problem. This could, as the framework suggests, call for empirical exploration rather than making assumptions in theory.

References

Almedom, A.M., 2005. Social capital and mental health: An interdisciplinary review of primary evidence. *Social Science and Medicine*, 61(5), pp. 943–64.

Arah, O.A., 2008. Effect of vote abstention and life course socio-economic position on self-reported health. *Journal of Epidemiology and Community Health*, 62(8), pp. 759–60.

Baybeck, B. and McClurg, S.D., 2005. What do they know and how do they know it? Citizen awareness of local context. *American Politics Research*, 33(4), pp. 492–520.

Bazargan, M., Kang, T.S. and Bazargan, S., 1991. A multivariate comparison of elderly African Americans' and Caucasians' voting behavior: How do social, health, psychological, and political variables affect their voting? *The International Journal of Aging and Human Development*, 32(3), pp. 181–98.

Beaudoin, C.E. and Thorson, E., 2004. Social capital in rural and urban communities: Testing differences in media effects and models. *Journalism and Mass Communication Quarterly*, 81(2), pp. 378–99.

Bhatti, Y. and Hansen, K.M., 2012. Retiring from voting: Turnout among senior voters. *Journal of Elections, Public Opinion and Parties*, 22(4), pp. 479–500.

Blakely, T.A., Kennedy, B.P. and Kawachi, I., 2001. Socioeconomic inequality in voting participation and self-rated health. *American Journal of Public Health*, 91(1), pp. 99–104.

Brody, R. and Sniderman, P., 1977. From life space to polling place: The relevance of personal concerns for voting behavior. *British Journal of Political Science*, 7(3), pp. 337–60.

Bryngelsson, A., 2009. Long-term sickness absence and social exclusion. *Scandinavian Journal of Public Health*, 37(8), pp. 839–45.

Bukov, A., Maas, I. and Lampert, T., 2002. Social participation in very old age: Cross-sectional and longitudinal findings from BASE. *The Journals of Gerontology Series B Psychological Sciences and Social Sciences*, 57(6), pp. 510–17.

Burden, B.C., Fletcher, J., Herd, P., Moynihan, D.P. and Jones, B.M., 2017. How different forms of health matter to political participation. *Journal of Politics*, 79(1), pp. 166–78.

Chan, K. and Chiu, M., 2007. The politics of citizenship formation: Political participation of mental health service users in Hong Kong. *Asian Journal of Social Science*, 35(2), pp. 195–215.

Cockerham, W.C., Hinote, B.P., Cockerham, G.B. and Abbott, P., 2006. Health lifestyles and political ideology in Belarus, Russia, and Ukraine. *Social Science and Medicine*, 62(7), pp. 1799–809.

Cummins, S., Stafford, M., Macintyre, S., Marmot, M. and Ellaway, A., 2005. Neighbourhood environment and its association with self rated health: Evidence from Scotland and England. *Journal of Epidemiology and Community Health*, 59(3), pp. 207–13.

Davey Smith, G. and Dorling, D., 1996. I'm all right John: Voting patterns and mortality in England and Wales, 1981–92. *British Medical Journal*, 313(7072), pp. 1573–7.

Denny, K. and Doyle, O., 2007a. Analysing the relationship between voter turnout and health in Ireland. *Irish Medical Journal*, 100(8), pp. 56–8.

Denny, K. and Doyle, O., 2007b. Take up thy bed, and vote: Measuring the relationship between voting behavior and indicators of health. *European Journal of Public Health*, 17(4), pp. 400–1.

Denny, K. and Doyle, O., 2009. Does voting history matter? Analyzing persistence in turnout source. *American Journal of Political Science*, 53(1), pp. 10–17.

d'Hombres, B., Rocco, L., Suhrcke, M. and McKee, M., 2010. Does social capital determine health? Evidence from eight transition countries. *Health Economics*, 19(1), pp. 56–74.

Dorling, D., Davey-Smith, G. and Shaw, M., 2001. Analysis of trends in premature mortality by Labour voting in the 1997 general election. *British Medical Journal*, 322(7298), pp. 1336–7.

Gabriel, O.W., 2012. Cognitive political engagement. In S.I. Keil and O.W. Gabriel, eds. *Society and democracy in Europe*. Abingdon: Routledge, pp. 162–84.

Gastil, J., 2000. The political beliefs and orientations of people with disabilities. *Social Science Quarterly*, 81(2), pp. 588–603.

Gleason, S., 2001. Female political participation and health in India. *Annals of the American Academy of Political and Social Science*, 573, pp. 105–26.

Goerres, A., 2006. Why are older people more likely to vote? The impact of ageing on electoral turnout in Europe. *The British Journal of Politics and International Relations*, 9(1), pp. 90–121.

Gollust, S. and Rahn, W., 2015. The bodies politic: Chronic health conditions and voter turnout in the 2008 election. *Journal of Health Politics, Policy and Law*, 40(6), pp. 1115–55.

Gustafsson, K., Aronsson, G., Marklund, S., Wikman, A. and Floderus, B., 2013. Does social isolation and low societal participation predict disability pension? A population based study. *PLoS One*, 8(11), p. e80655.

Hassell, H. and Settle, J.E., 2017. The differential effects of stress on voter turnout. *Political Psychology*, 38(3), 533–50.

Huijts, T., Perkins, J. and Subramanian, S.V., 2010. Political regimes, political ideology, and self-rated health in Europe: A multilevel analysis. *PLoS One*, 5(7), pp. e11711.

Hyyppä, M. and Mäki, J., 2003. Social participation and health in a community rich in stock of social capital. *Health Education Research*, 18(6), pp. 770–9.

Islam, K.M., Merlo, J., Kawachi, I., Lindström, M. and Gerdtham, U., 2006. Social capital and health: Does egalitarianism matter? A literature review. *International Journal for Equity in Health*, 5(1), p. 3.

Karp, J. and Banducci, S., 2001. Absentee voting, mobilization, and participation. *American Politics Research*, 29(2), pp. 183–95.

Kawachi, I., Kennedy, B.P., Gupta, V. and Prothrow-Stith, D., 1999. Women's status and the health of women and men: A view from the States. *Social Science and Medicine*, 48(1), pp. 21–32.

Kelleher, C., Timoney, A., Friel, S. and McKeown, D., 2002. Indicators of deprivation, voting patterns, and health status at area level in the Republic of Ireland. *Journal of Epidemiology and Community Health*, 56(1), pp. 36–44.

Kondrichin, S.V. and Lester, D., 1998. Voting conservative and mortality. *Perceptual and Motor Skills*, 87(2), p. 466.

Kondrichin, S.V. and Lester, D., 1999. "I'm all right Jack" in Russia too. *Perceptual and Motor Skills*, 88(3), p. 892.

Lahtinen, H., Mattila, M., Wass, H. and Martikainen, P., 2017. Explaining social-class inequality in voter turnout: the contribution of income and health. *Scandinavian Political Studies*, in press.

Macinko, J. and Starfield, B., 2001. The utility of social capital in research on health determinants. *Milbank Quarterly*, 79(3), pp. 387–427.

MacKenbach, J.P. and McKee, M., 2013. Social-democratic government and health policy in Europe: A quantitative analysis. *International Journal of Health Services*, 43(3), pp. 389–413.

Matsubayashi, T. and Ueda, M., 2014. Disability and voting. *Disability and Health Journal*, 7(3), pp. 285–91.

Mattila, M. and Papageorgiou, A., 2016. Disability, perceived discrimination and political participation. *International Political Science Review*.

Mattila, M., Söderlund, P., Wass, H. and Rapeli, L., 2013. Healthy voting: The effect of self-reported health on turnout in 30 countries. *Electoral Studies*, 32(4), pp. 886–91.

McClurg, S.D., 2003. Social networks and political participation: The role of social interaction in explaining political participation. *Political Research Quarterly*, 56(4), pp. 448–64.

Melucci, A., 1996. *Challenging codes: Collective action in the information age*. Cambridge University Press: Cambridge.

Miller, P. and Powell, S., 2016. Overcoming voting obstacles: The use of convenience voting by voters with disabilities. *American Politics Research*, 44(1), pp. 28–55.

Navarro, V., Borrell, C., Benach, J., Muntaner, C., Quiroga, A., Rodríguez-Sanz, M., Vergés, N., Gumá, J. and Pasarín, M.I., 2003. The importance of the political and the social in explaining mortality differentials among the countries of the OECD, 1950–1998. *International Journal of Health Services*, 33(3), pp. 419–94.

Navarro, V., Muntaner, C., Borrell, C., Benach, J., Quiroga, Á., Rodríguez-Sanz, M., Vergés, N. and Pasarín, M.I., 2006. Politics and health outcomes. *Lancet*, 368(9540), pp. 1033–7.

Nygård, M. and Jakobsson, G., 2013. Political participation of older adults in Scandinavia – the civic voluntarism model revisited? A multi-level analysis of three types of political participation. *International Journal of Ageing and Later Life*, 8(1), pp. 65–96.

Ojeda, C., 2015. Depression and political participation. *Social Science Quarterly*, 96(5), pp. 1226–43.

Pacheco, J. and Fletcher, J., 2015. Incorporating health into studies of political behavior: Evidence for turnout and partisanship. *Political Research Quarterly*, 68(1), pp. 104–16.

Page, A., Morrell, S. and Taylor, R., 2002. Suicide and political regime in New South Wales and Australia during the 20th century. *Journal of Epidemiology and Community Health*, 56(10), pp. 766–72.

Peterson, S.A., 1987. Biosocial predictors of older Americans' political participation. *Politics and the Life Sciences*, 5(2), pp. 246–54.

Peterson, S.A., 1990. *Political behavior: Patterns in everyday life*. Newbury Park: Sage.

Polletta, F. and Jasper, J.M., 2001. Collective identity and social movements. *Annual Review of Sociology*, 27, pp. 283–305.

Putnam, R.D., 2000. *Bowling alone: The collapse and revival of American community*. New York: Simon & Schuster.

Reitan, T.C., 2003. Too sick to vote? Public health and voter turnout in Russia during the 1990s. *Communist and Post-Communist Studies*, 36(1), pp. 49–68.

Schur, L. and Adya, M., 2012. Sidelined or mainstreamed? Political participation and attitudes of people with disabilities in the United States. *Social Science Quarterly*, 94(3), pp. 811–39.

Schur, L., Adya, M. and Kruse, D., 2013. *Disability, voter turnout, and voting difficulties in the 2012 elections*. Report to the U.S. Election Assistance Commission and Research Alliance for Accessible Voting.

Schur, L.A. and Kruse, D.L., 2000. What determines voter turnout? Lessons from citizens with disabilities. *Social Science Quarterly*, 81(2), pp. 571–87.

Schur, L., Shields, T., Kruse, D. and Schriner, K., 2002. Enabling democracy: disability and voter turnout. *Political Research Quarterly*, 55:1, 167–90.

Schur, L., Shields, T. and Schriner, K., 2003. Can I make a difference? Efficacy, employment, and disability. *Political Psychology*, 24(1), pp. 119–49.

Schur, L., Shields, T. and Schriner, K., 2005a. Generational cohorts, group membership, and political participation by people with disabilities. *Political Research Quarterly*, 58(3), pp. 487–96.

Schur, L., Shields, T. and Schriner, K., 2005b. Voting. In Gary Albrecht, ed. *Encyclopedia of disability*. Thousand Oaks: Sage, pp. 1615–19.

Sears, D.O. and Funk, C.L., 1991. The role of self-interest in social and political attitudes. *Advances in Experimental Social Psychology*, 24, pp. 1–91.

Shaw, M., Dorling, D. and Davey Smith, G., 2002. Editorial: Mortality and political climate: How suicide rates have risen during periods of conservative government, 1901–2000. *Journal of Epidemiology and Community Health*, 56(10), pp. 722–7.

Shin, M.E. and McCarthy, W.J., 2013. The association between county political inclination and obesity: Results from the 2012 presidential election in the United States. *Preventive Medicine*, 57(5), pp. 721–4.

Söderlund, P. and Rapeli, L., 2015. In sickness and in health: Personal health and political participation in the Nordic countries. *Politics and the Life Sciences*, 34(1), pp. 28–43.

Solt, F., 2008. Economic inequality and democratic political engagement. *American Journal of Political Science*, 52(1), pp. 48–60.

Subramanian, S.V., Hamano, T., Perkins, J.M., Koyabu, A. and Fujisawa, Y., 2010. Political ideology and health in Japan: A disaggregated analysis. *Journal of Epidemiology and Community Health*, 64(9), pp. 838–40.

Subramanian, S.V., Huijts, T. and Perkins, J.M., 2009. Association between political ideology and health in Europe. *European Journal of Public Health*, 19(5), pp. 455–7.

Subramanian, S.V. and Perkins, J.M., 2010. Are Republicans healthier than Democrats? *International Journal of Epidemiology*, 39(3), pp. 930–1.

Sund, R., Lahtinen, H., Wass, H., Mattila, M. and Martikainen, P., 2017. How voter turnout varies between different chronic conditions? *Journal of Epidemiology and Community Health*, 71(5), 475–79.

Sundquist, K. and Yang, M., 2007. Linking social capital and self-rated health: A multilevel analysis of 11,175 men and women in Sweden. *Health and Place*, 13(2), pp. 324–34.

Timpone, R., 1998. Structure, behavior and voter turnout in the United States. *American Political Science Review*, 92(1), pp. 145–58.

Urbatsch, R., 2017. Influenza and voter turnout. *Scandinavian Political Studies* 40(1): 107–119

Verba, S., Schlozman, K.L. and Brady, H., 1995. *Voice and equality: Civic voluntarism in American politics*. Cambridge: Harvard University Press.

Wass, H., Mattila, M., Rapeli, L. and Söderlund. P., 2017. Voting while ailing? The effect of voter facilitation instruments on health-related differences in turnout. *Journal of Elections, Public Opinion and Parties*, forthcoming.

Whooley, O., 2007. Collective identity. In G. Ritzer, ed. *Blackwell encyclopaedia of sociology online* (last visited on 25 November 2016).

3 Health and political participation

Introduction

Unequally distributed political participation continues to represent one of the unresolved democratic dilemmas. As Chalmers (2016, 2) points out, "the idea that everyone is represented in a democratic system has been widely proclaimed and celebrated, yet dramatic inequality is notable in income, education, healthcare, financial security, and many other dimensions." Not only is political participation and representation systematically skewed in favour of better- educated, more affluent and healthier citizens (for a review, see Wass and Blais, 2017), the output of political decision-making processes also better corresponds with the interests of wealthier citizens (e.g., Butler, 2014; Enns and Wlezien, 2011; Gilens, 2012).

In this chapter, we examine the extent to which health constitutes a factor that contributes to inequalities in political participation. Poor health or functional limitations may influence all components in Verba, Schlozman and Brady's (1995, pp. 16–17) civic voluntarism model, i.e., resources, motivation and mobilization by churches, voluntary associations, informal social networks and political organizations, as health problems often hamper involvement in social activities and group meetings (e.g., Schur, Kruse and Blanck, 2013, pp. 130–1). However, the barriers to participation due to ill health are not only concerns for an individual. According to the 'social model of disability', health impairment (an aspect of an individual) becomes a disability only when it interacts with unfavourable circumstances in his/her surroundings (ibid., pp. 9–10). In an inclusive democracy, practices for political participation should be accessible for all kinds of citizens, regardless of their resources or personal characteristics.

In some cases, however, poor health or disability can actually have an activating effect on participation (Gollust and Rahn, 2015; Mattila and Papageorgiou, 2016; Söderlund and Rapeli, 2015; Sund et al., 2017). This may be due to mechanisms such as self-interest in elections, particularly when healthcare issues are politicized; active membership in patient associations, which construct social identity as well as provide venues for mobilization; and resentment (a feeling that the group is treated unfairly) as a trigger for collective action (Denny and Doyle, 2007b; Gollust and Rahn, 2015, 1121–4; Mattila and Papageorgiou, 2016, 3; Söderlund and Rapeli, 2015).

In what follows, we briefly review the existing studies of health and political participation using the funnel model of participation (Wass and Blais, 2017, p. 463) as an overarching framework (Figure 3.1). In the empirical analyses, we examine how two indicators of health – self-rated health (SRH) and disability – are linked to six forms of political participation. As Burden et al. (2017, 176) acknowledge, "both health and political participation have multiple dimensions, so any claim such as 'health matters' is bound to be simplistic." Our objective is thus to approach the health–participation link from several angles. We conclude by discussing the role of health as a resource for political action.

Health in the funnel model of political participation

Our understanding of political participation has expanded substantially over several decades, from voting and other types of 'conventional participation' (contacting officials, signing petitions) to protests and social movements, and, more recently, to social engagement and civic participation (Amnå and Ekman, 2014, p. 269). Several criteria can be used to categorize these various participation forms, such as parliamentary/conventional vs. non-parliamentary/unconventional, collective vs. individualist, and organizational vs. grassroots engagement. All of these, however, share certain characteristics. Teorell et al. (2007) identify four common components of political participation, including (1) action undertaken by individuals (2) who are ordinary citizens, (3) with the intention to influence decisions taken by others (beyond everyday discussions and political interest) and (4) related to any political outcome in society (not only decisions made by public representatives and officials).

Despite some early interest in the connection between health and turnout on the part of political scientists (for a review, see Blank and Hines, 2001, pp. 91–3; Peterson, 1990, pp. 82–6), the topic has only attracted more attention from scholars working in health-related fields in recent times. A number of recent studies have reported relationships between physical or mental health and voting. For instance, people with poor general and mental health have been shown to vote less in general elections in Britain and Ireland (Denny and Doyle, 2007a, b). A series of analyses has shown that people with disabilities are less likely to vote in US elections (e.g., Miller and Powell, 2016; Schur and Adya, 2013; Schur and Kruse, 2000, 2014; Schur, Kruse and Blanck, 2013; Schur et al. 2002; Shields et al., 1998a, b; for a review, see Ward, Baker and Moon, 2009). A region-level analysis of turnout in Russia, meanwhile, suggested that low turnout was associated with shorter average life expectancy (Reitan, 2003). Finally, a Swedish study, which explored the association between long-term sickness absence and non-voting, found that the effect of sickness absence was not significant, possibly due to a small number of observations (Bryngelson, 2009).

The upper level includes the effects of institutional and contextual characteristics, which may be mediated by more proximate individual-level factors or moderate their impact. This block dictates the overall setting where political participation takes place. A wide conceptualization of this system level is particularly

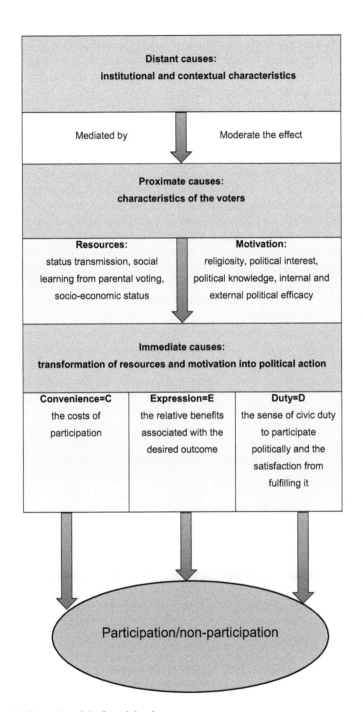

Figure 3.1 Funnel model of participation

Source: Wass and Blais, 2017, p. 463 (with modifications).

important in association with health. Inclusive democracy cannot simply limit the structures of a political system. As political participation reflects individuals' levels of cognitive, physical, economic and social resources, policies with a bearing on health, jobs or income redistribution are equally as important as electoral engineering, if not more so (see Norris, 2004).

The institutional level has, so far, remained undiscovered territory in studies of the health–participation relationship. The most comprehensive account is introduced in Chapter 6 of this book, showing that four contextual factors predict smaller turnout gaps between health groups: compulsory voting, party-centred electoral systems, higher density of trade unions, and a greater share of left-wing parties. However, there are also other characteristics that might prove to be important. An interesting, although not yet explored, issue relates to the role of economic inequality, i.e., the question as to whether health-related inequalities in electoral participation are more or less pronounced in countries with a more egalitarian welfare system. While generous welfare provision could narrow participation gaps between the healthy and the unhealthy by equalizing opportunities and lowering the costs of participation, it is also possible that a lack of adequate social support could narrow health-related participation gaps in less generous welfare systems by mobilizing citizens with poor health. Denny and Doyle (2007a) uncovered an interaction between poor health and dissatisfaction with the Irish health service: people with poor health were actually more likely to vote if they were dissatisfied with the health service.

The middle part of the funnel model in Figure 3.1 addresses individual-level characteristics, which are considered more proximate causes of participation. Here, the connection in the civic voluntarism model (Verba, Schlozman and Brady, 1995, pp. 16–17) becomes evident (see also Verba et al., 1995). As mentioned in the previous section, health has an impact on all of the three reasons why people take part in politics: because they can (resources), because they want to (motivation) and because they were asked to (mobilization). In the funnel model of participation, mobilization is included among the distant causes of institutional and contextual characteristics, while resources and motivation are considered equally important proximate causes (Wass and Blais, 2017, p. 464).

In terms of resources, poor health or disability expectedly have negative implications. They may hinder the acquisition of adequate skills, time and money, all of which are considered essential resources for political participation (Verba, Schlozman and Brady, 1995, p. 16; see also Schur, Kruse and Blanck, 2013, p. 92). Experienced particularly at a young age, poor health could lead to lower levels of employment and income (Adler and Ostrove, 1999). However, the lack of economic inclusion extends way beyond money to involve social and psychological aspects (Schur, Kruse and Blanck, 2013, p. 27). For instance, unemployment is not only an economic hurdle, but also prevents engagement in community, recreational and political activities outside the workplace (ibid.). It is also worth noting that the negative effect of health problems on participatory resources may also affect others as well as those who are themselves concerned: care-givers are involved in nursing or taking over tasks that are normally handled by the person suffering the illness (Urbatsch, 2017).

While health problems or functional disabilities may jeopardize the acquisition of other politically relevant resources, health may also constitute a resource in its own right. Priestley et al. (2016, p. 2) argue that "there is a strong case that disability equality should be considered along with other socio-economic variables when researching political participation, but there are unique dimensions to consider too." The fact that the link between health and participation can be traced back to adolescence seems to support the interpretation of health as an independent pre-adult resource (Pacheco and Fletcher, 2015, p. 106). Using the data from the National Longitudinal Study of Adolescent Health, Pacheco and Fletcher (2015) show that, even after controlling for socio-economic status and other relevant correlates, an adolescent with excellent health has a 7 percentage point higher probability of voting five years later than his/her peers with poor health.

The effect of ill health on the other proximate cause for political participation, namely motivation, is less straightforward. On the one hand, citizens with ill health may be less motivated to participate in politics due to a lower sense of political efficacy and because dealing with their condition requires a lot of mental effort, which can reduce their capacity to follow politics (Denny and Doyle, 2007a; Schur, Kruse and Blanck, 2013, 93). Some conditions may even have a direct association with motivation towards political action. For example, Ojeda (2015) shows that depression suppresses turnout, even after controlling for socio-demographic characteristics, church attendance, the strength of partisanship, general health and happiness. Moreover, the negative effect of adolescent depressed mood is partially mediated through educational attainment and party identification, while weakly mediated through social interaction with friends.

Yet, there is another side to this story. Söderlund and Rapeli (2015) found that poor SRH in fact mobilizes participation in certain types of activities, such as wearing a campaign badge/sticker, contacting a politician or public official, and taking part in a lawful demonstration. The authors suggest that this is due to two mechanisms (ibid., 36). On the one hand, people with ill health may prefer activities that are most easily undertaken, such as wearing a political badge. On the other hand, because they have so much at stake, they might actively try to influence policymaking and thus select a high investment–high payoff strategy.

Surprisingly perhaps, some chronic conditions seem to have an activating impact as well. A US study indicates that, after adjusting for socio-demographic characteristics and some health-related confounding factors, voters with a cancer diagnosis are more likely to vote (Gollust and Rahn, 2015). The authors are mindful that this effect stems from the de-stigmatized character of how cancer is perceived in society (e.g., former patients are often portrayed as heroic survivors, rather than as responsible for their condition) and the high membership rate of influential cancer-patient associations. Associations have multiple roles: constructing a social identity that aims to transform illness-caused marginalization into a collective resource based on a shared experience, as well as providing venues for mobilization and participation, which can, in turn, develop civic skills to facilitate political engagement, especially among those with a disadvantaged educational or ethnic background. Correspondingly, a Finnish study based on individual-level register-based data (Sund et al. 2017) discovered a positive association between cancer and voting.[1]

Meanwhile, Mattila and Papageorgiou (2016) discovered that, although disability is associated with lower turnout, it has the opposite effect on taking part in demonstrations and contacting politicians or government officials. As in the case of chronic diseases, the activating mechanism may be traced back to group identity: people do not demonstrate or contact politicians in order to secure or restore their private benefits, but to promote collective interests. Unlike voting, such forms of participation enable the group to set the agenda, especially if the promoted issue does not fall within the boundaries of mainstream political discourse.

The lower part of the funnel model in Figure 3.1 includes three reasons as to why citizens choose to take part in political action: because it is easy or convenient, because they want to express an opinion, and because they feel they should. These three components have a connection with the rational choice model of voting, i.e., costs, benefits and duty (Wass and Blais, 2017, p. 464).[2] In relation to health, the costs, particularly the attempts to reduce them, probably represent the most noteworthy factor. As Miller and Powell (2016, p. 29) remark: "Voting is a costly activity, but these costs are not equal to all voters. A voter must both negotiate a bureaucratic process and process information accumulated in the course of [a] campaign to cast her ballot." Priestly et al. (2016, 7) make a corresponding argument by dividing accessibility in elections into two components, namely, access to information (forms of communication designed to ensure participation for disabled people, particularly with sensory or cognitive impairments) and access to a polling station.

There are multiple potential mechanisms linking health-related complications with costs of or, more precisely, barriers to participation. Voters with mobility, visual, auditory, cognitive or manual dexterity impairments may experience different kinds of obstacles (Tokaji and Colker, 2007, p. 1030). In general, voters suffering from functional limitations are also more affected by those factors that increase the costs of voting for all citizens, such as long lines (Schur, Adya and Kruse, 2013). In a survey conducted after the 2012 US elections, the most common obstacles mentioned by voters with disabilities were difficulty in reading or seeing the ballot (12 per cent), understanding how to vote or use the voting equipment (10 per cent), waiting in line (8 per cent), finding or getting to the polling station (6 per cent), writing on the ballot (5 per cent), and accessing the polling station (4 per cent) (ibid.). Voters with disabilities may also be discouraged by interactions with poll workers who lack adequate knowledge to deal with disabilities or offer assistance (Ward, Baker and Moon, 2009, p. 80; see also Schur, Kruse and Blanck, 2013, p. 108).

Even wider environmental factors can make a difference in terms of participation costs. Clarke et al. (2011) found that voters with difficulties in mobility had a considerably lower propensity to vote when they resided in areas characterized by poor street conditions, whereas good conditions acted as a leveller between voters with and without mobility impairments.

In order to compensate for the uneven costs of participation by decreasing practical barriers, many countries have implemented various types of voter facilitation procedures. Such facilitation instruments, including advance voting, absentee voting, assisted voting, proxy voting and mobile voting stations, specifically to promote voting in hospitals and other institutions (Karlawish and Bonnie, 2007, 885), are expected to increase not only participation but also the socio-economic representativeness of the electorate, balancing out different sorts of bias in turnout (e.g., Berinsky, 2005, p. 471; Karp and Banducci, 2000, pp. 223–4; Tokaji and Colker, 2007, 1023).

In practice, voter facilitation instruments have shown only a limited capability to narrow health-related differences in participation. By differentiating between mail voting and in-person early voting, Alvarez and his colleagues (2012) discovered that older and disabled voters had a lower propensity to vote on election day than in advance. In addition, disability increased the tendency to vote by mail. Miller and Powell (2016, 48) summarized their findings from the US context in a similar vein: "There is little evidence to suggest voters with a disability cast their ballots at the polling place on Election Day. Instead, these data show voters with a disability in large part cast mail ballots."

Schur and Kruse (2014) also found that, in the US context, turnout was substantially higher among four disability groups (hearing, visual and mobility impairments, and difficulty going outside) in all vote-by-mail states than in states where voting by mail must be requested. Vote-by-mail systems were also found to reduce the likelihood among voters with disabilities to not vote because of illness or disability. Full online registration increased the voting propensity among voters with cognitive impairments, while election day registration had a corresponding effect only among people with hearing impairments and without disabilities. Rather surprisingly, devices to assist voting by people with disabilities did not have a significant impact, whereas the availability of early voting in fact decreased the likelihood of voting among those hampered by cognitive or mobility impairments.

Using European Social Survey (ESS) data, Wass et al. (2017) examined the extent to which voter facilitation policies reduced health-related bias in voting. Their analysis, which encompassed an 11-year period and 30 countries, revealed that not only were the main effects of voter facilitation insignificant, but health-related inequalities in turnout were exacerbated in those countries where the strongest efforts are made to ensure accessible voting. The authors interpreted these findings, which at first glance are cause for some surprise and even dismay, as supporting the reverse causation or endogeneity argument. Those countries with the sharpest differences in turnout rates between different social groups have been more likely to implement voter facilitation instruments to remedy such skews. Where inequalities have consistently been less pronounced, there has been no urgency to make voting more convenient.

Poor health or disability may also weaken the two other components of immediate causes for participation, i.e., perceived benefits and citizen duty. A diminished sense of political efficacy and a lower level of political trust may function as concrete mechanisms linking health to participation. If voters feel unable to communicate their needs and preferences to the government or if the government is unable or unwilling to respond to them, expected benefits from political participation, as well as the sense of obligation to participate, may weaken. There is some evidence of a connection between health, lower levels of political efficacy and perceived government responsiveness among people with disabilities (Gastil, 2000; Schur and Adya, 2013).

Theoretical expectations

As the preceding literature review indicated, theories of political participation offer competing views of how health problems could plausibly affect levels of political activity. A straightforward reading of resource theory certainly seems to suggest a negative impact, i.e., that experiencing health problems leads to diminished political activity, as Hypothesis 1 in Chapter 2 assumed. Health problems can be seen as a burden that diminishes those psychological, as well as other, resources which support political engagement.

On the other hand, people who have lived with a chronic health condition, at least since adolescence, may not consider their health problem to be a factor that depresses political engagement. For them, a health problem may not feel like a reason to withdraw from politics, but more like a feature of everyday life. For those who start experiencing health problems later in life, when they have already established certain patterns and levels of political participation, such issues may feel like an obstacle to engagement (Hypothesis 2). Hence we assume that perceiving poor health as a lack of resource may depend on the timing as to when health started affecting a person's life.

Whereas resource theory fundamentally suggests that poor health negatively affects engagement, self-interest theory leads to opposite conclusions. From a self-interest viewpoint, personal health can be seen as a source of motivation for people experiencing health problems. Such people have unusually high stakes in policy debates because, in many cases, they depend on public health services. The incentive to know what is going on in politics and support a certain party or candidate is therefore much higher than for other people, with no particularly strong need for specific policy outcomes.

In general terms, self-interest theory predicts that health problems, unless they are so severe that they make political engagement practically impossible, increase political participation (Hypothesis 3). Meanwhile, socio-economic status could constitute a conditioning variable: the extent to which a person with health problems relies on public healthcare probably depends on personal finances. People with economic independence from the public sector may not experience a heightened sense of motivation to participate in politics, even if they might benefit from certain policy outputs.

Following Söderlund and Rapeli (2015), we also test a hypothesis concerning the varying impact of health between different forms of participation. What they called 'the convenience hypothesis' suggests that "people with poor health, relatively speaking, will participate more actively through forms of involvement that pose fewer concrete obstacles, such as wearing a campaign badge, boycotting products, or signing a petition" (Söderlund and Rapeli, 2015, p. 32). Furthermore, this logic emanates from the resource model: as ill health typically diminishes resources for political engagement, those who are experiencing health problems are likely to choose forms of participation that are most easily accessible.

Analysis

In order to test our three hypotheses, we use a total of six different forms of political participation and two indicators of health, i.e., SRH and disability. In addition to voting in the 2015 parliamentary election, the respondents were asked, from among a number of participation forms, which they had been involved with during the past 12 months. Out of eight alternatives, five were included in the analysis: contacting a politician or public official, working for an organization or association besides a political party, signing a petition, boycotting a product, and expressing a political opinion on social media. Participation in a legal demonstration, working for a political party and wearing a campaign product or badge were excluded, due to the small number of respondents reporting these activities.

As the analyses cover multiple dependent and independent variables in several statistical models (baseline/full), we only report the main findings as predicted probabilities. These are based on full models including gender, age, age squared, education, income, marital status and life situation. The coding of these variables is presented in Chapter 2.

The results presented in Figure 3.2 lend support to Hypothesis 1. The likelihood of participating tends to be lower among people who rate their health as fair or poor. From the point of view of resource theory, it is safe to conclude that health problems diminish psychological and material resources, which are conducive for political participation. The difference between health groups is, however, smallest for voting, which is the most pivotal form of participation. The differences are also modest for contacting a politician or public official and participation in organizations and associations.

However, we could not replicate the findings by Söderlund and Rapeli (2015), namely, that people with health problems choose more convenient modes of participation. In contrast to what was suggested by Hypothesis 3, our analysis shows a rather stable pattern of diminished participation across all participatory forms. In this respect, the results are, to a large extent, in line with those derived from the Finnish National Election Study (FNES) 2015 data (see Mattila et al., 2016, pp. 428–9).

Figure 3.3 illustrates the results from identical analyses using disability as the indicator of health. The results clearly contrast with those derived on the basis of SRH. People who report not being at all hampered in their daily lives by a disability show the lowest rates of political participation on all counts besides voting; in such cases, differences are insignificant. Additionally, citizens who are most hampered by a disability are most active in terms of contacting a politician or a public official and signing a petition. This not only contradicts Hypothesis 1,

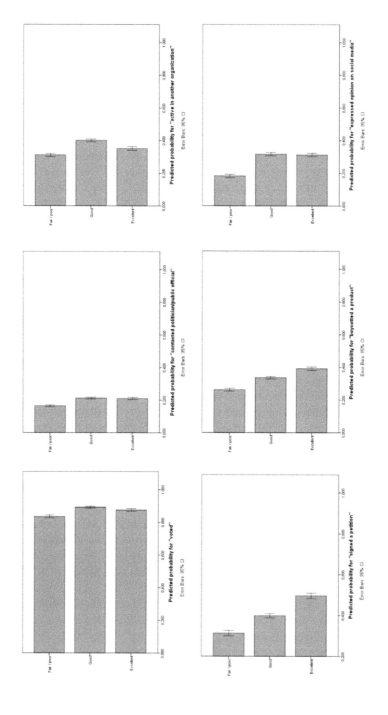

Figure 3.2 Predicted probabilities for different forms of political participation by SRH

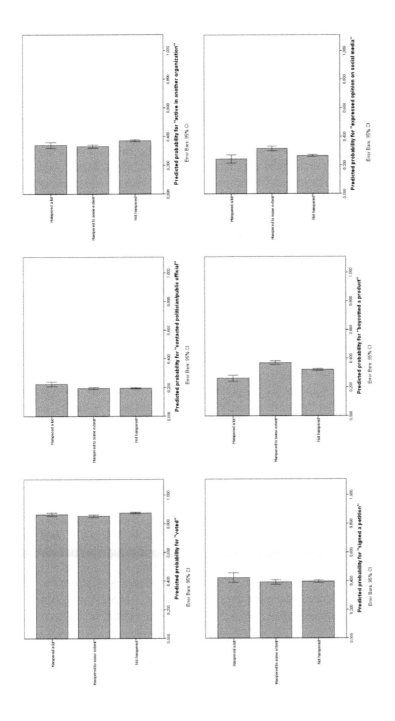

Figure 3.3 Predicted probabilities for different forms of political participation by disability

it also provides partial support for the convenience hypothesis put forward by Söderlund and Rapeli (2015), given that signing a petition may be considered a highly convenient way of participating.

The finding that people with a disability are active in contacting decision makers can be seen as supporting another assumption from Söderlund and Rapeli (2015). What was labelled as the 'increased activism hypothesis' suggests that heightened self-interest when it comes to favourable policy outcomes could motivate people with health problems to choose forms of participation that are potentially more effective than, say, voting or signing a petition. Direct contact with decision makers is certainly a form of participation that can have more immediate consequences than many others. In other words, there are indications that motivation levels for political participation are, in many cases, higher among people suffering from a disability than among those who have good health.

Addressing Hypothesis 2, which suggests that health problems negatively impact participation to a greater degree when experienced later in the life cycle, we repeated the same analyses and compared those respondents who have suffered from health problems since childhood or adolescence with respondents who started experiencing health problems later in life. The results reported in Figure 3.4 include those of the 690 respondents who said they were hampered either a lot or to some extent in their daily activities by a long-standing illness, disability, infirmity or mental health problem.

Our assumption that participation rates would be lower among those whose health problems had started after the formation of political behaviour patterns gains partial support (Figure 3.4). In the case of signing a petition, boycotting a product and expressing political opinions on social media, our expectations are confirmed: i.e., that those whose daily lives were hampered by health problems from an early phase in the life cycle are significantly more active. For the other forms of participation, the opposite holds.

This mixture of mutually inconclusive empirical observations does not easily render itself to interpretation. It seems as if those who have suffered from a health problem since childhood or adolescence overwhelmingly choose modes of participation that can be considered convenient and easily accessible. Those whose problems started later in life more often choose forms that are considered conventional, namely, voting and contacting politicians or public officials. If health problems begin affecting daily activities later in life, people may also be more likely to use more efficient and direct forms of participation when they suddenly find themselves dependent on the political system for healthcare services. Those who have lived their entire lives, more or less, coping with a health problem may feel more motivated towards engaging in politics through alternative, unconventional ways as well. These findings are not, however, explained by the possibility that the survey respondents who have suffered from a health problem since very early on in their lives just happened to be younger than the rest, meaning that they are more likely to engage in new, alternative forms of participation. In fact, those who report a health problem that has endured since childhood or adolescence are, on average, six years older than those who do not. Although we cannot conclusively

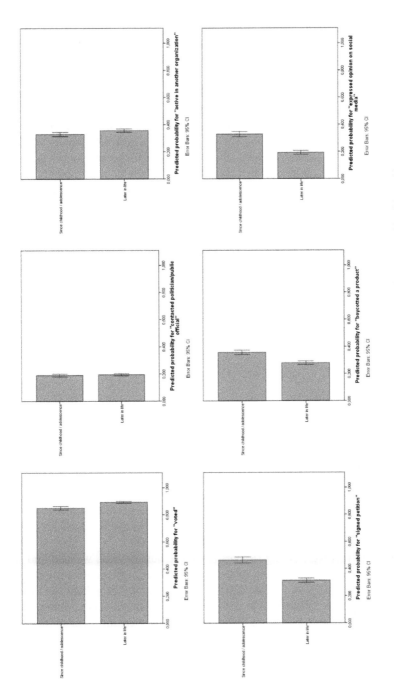

Figure 3.4 Predicted probabilities for different forms of political participation by timing of the start of health problems

interpret this particular observation, we can exclude the possibility of it being a simple artefact of respondent demographics.

Finally, we consider the related possibility that a person's economic status influences the relationship between health and political participation. The logic here is that personal economic insecurity makes citizens more likely to rely on public healthcare, thereby increasing their motivation to participate in politics. To test this hypothesis, we run the same analyses and report the predicted probabilities for each form of participation for two groups: (1) those with poor health or disability and low income and (2) those with poor health or disability and high income. To divide the respondents into low and high income groups, we use a continuous income variable, which takes into consideration total monthly family income, controlling for the number of minors living in the same household. The lowest 30 percent represents the low income group, while the highest 30 percent represents the high income group.

The results in Figures 3.5 and 3.6 convincingly reject this hypothesis. Rather than having a mobilizing effect, as suggested by self-interest theory, the combination of poor health or disability and low income is consistently associated with lower rates of participation, compared with respondents with similar health problems and high income. This is particularly evident in the case of SRH (Figure 3.5). Voting is the only exception, as the differences between the income groups are insignificant for both SRH and disability.

Conclusions

All things considered, we find more support for resource theory as an explanation for the relationship between health and political participation than for self-interest approaches. Although there are significant deviations from the pattern, poor health more often depresses political participation than encourages the mobilization to act, as the premises behind self-interest theory would suggest. On the basis of the analyses presented in this chapter, it seems reasonable to consider health in a similar way, given that resource theory has traditionally regarded other factors as affecting political engagement. Furthermore, personal health is another component in the complex equation involving various circumstances, which either increase or decrease the likelihood of engagement.

In spite of relatively strong support for the resource model, we also find several instances where poor health increases political activity, as predicted by self-interest theory. There was a particularly noticeable difference between the two measures of health. While people with poor SRH were politically more passive, those suffering from a long-term illness or disability were more active than their healthy counterparts on almost all counts. Our findings, therefore, are consistent with those of previous studies, which show that different types of health problems relate differently to political engagement (see Mattila et al., 2016; Mattila and Papageorgiou, 2016; Söderlund and Rapeli, 2015). According to our results, the character of a health condition seems essential in terms of the direction of the effect on political engagement.

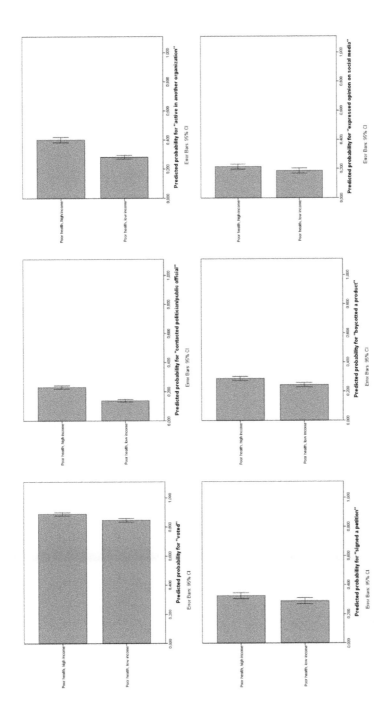

Figure 3.5 Predicted probabilities for different forms of participation by SRH and income

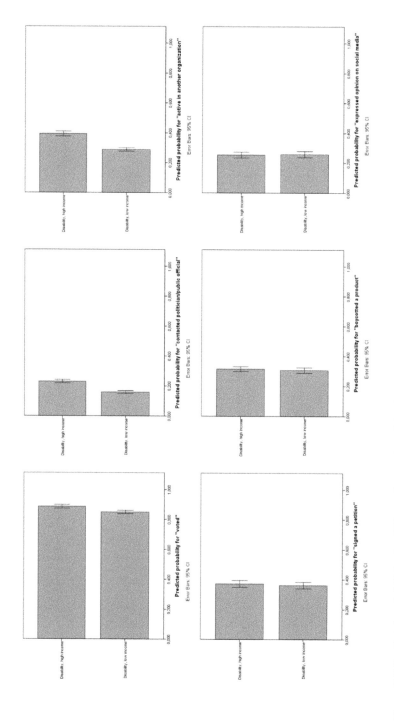

Figure 3.6 Predicted probabilities for different forms of participation by disability and income

Although a slightly speculative interpretation, it seems as if people with a chronic condition are often quite politically active because they might be more used to coping with their health problem. We find additional, but inconclusive, support for this contention when looking at how the beginning of health problems in different life stages relates to political action. The rates for signing a petition, boycotting a product or expressing a political opinion on social media are significantly higher for those whose lives have been affected by a long-term health problem since childhood or adolescence than for those who have had a similar problem much later in life. We interpret this at least as circumstantial evidence, showing that, if health problems are already affecting the everyday life of a person at a time when political behaviour patterns are developing, the impact of poor health is not necessarily negative. On the other hand, when health deteriorates later in life, it becomes more of a burden. The impact of 'diminished health resources' are therefore partly conditioned by the timing of health problems in the life cycle.

More evidence supporting the view that health is a resource comes from the final analysis in this chapter, which showed that, when combined with a disadvantaged economic position, low income only depresses participation. This could, of course, be a context-dependent matter. Finland is a highly equal society in terms of income differences, while the divide between reliance on the public healthcare system or the private sector is not particularly acute. It is quite possible that personal economics could even play a crucial role in determining the political behaviour of people in poor health in more economically divided societies.

This is a particularly noteworthy observation vis-à-vis the expectation that health may constitute a concrete mechanism, which leads to inequalities in political participation (see Chapter 1), particularly as the two are closely interrelated. Marmot (2015, p. 27) summarizes this quite aptly:

> The link between deprivation and life expectancy is remarkably graded: the greater the deprivation, the shorter your life expectancy. The social gradient in life expectancy runs all the way from top to bottom. It doesn't just feel better at the top. It *is* better. At the top, not only do you live longer but the quality of life is better – you spend more years free from disability.

The obvious next question concerns what can be done to compensate for such disadvantages and thus facilitate more equal participation. We have briefly addressed this issue in this chapter by reviewing the relatively discouraging findings from voter facilitation studies. It thus seems obvious that a one-size-fits-all approach is not an optimal way to reduce barriers to participation caused by health problems or disability. If the goal is to make participation more equal, it might be more effective to develop facilitation measures that are specifically suitable for voters with various types of special needs (Tokaji and Colker, 2007, p. 1017). There are many facilitation instruments to potentially mobilize voters with health impairments, which have not yet been empirically tested to a significant extent, such as online voting and ballots in Braille (Prince, 2014, p. 95). In addition, new computer technologies may improve conditions for political participation among voters with disabilities through increased access to information, networking and recruitment (Schur, Douglas and Blanck, 2013, p. 111).

Although there is still a long way to go in order to achieve full political inclusion (cf. ibid., p. 237), the development is nevertheless promising. These are also critical issues for the quality of democracy and citizenship. As Prince (2014, p. 114) points out, if voting requires disabled persons to ask for help from family or friends, the disability status is most likely to be perceived as a personal challenge, rather than a social issue and a problem of citizenship. Obviously, the same applies to people suffering from long-term or chronic illnesses.

Notes

1 However, the Finnish study was unable to replicate the interaction between the educational level and cancer: although it pointed in the same direction as Gollust and Rahn's study, suggesting that cancer has a particularly empowering effect among less-educated citizens, it was not statistically significant.
2 The P term (the probability of casting a decisive vote) is excluded from the original funnel model of voting, since it appears to be the least meaningful part of the voting calculus (see Wass and Blais, 2017, p. 464).

References

Adler, N.E. and Ostrove, J.M., 1999. Sosioeconomic status and health: What we know and what we don't. *Annals of the New York Academy of Sciences*, 896(1), pp. 3–15.

Alvarez, R.M., Levin, I. and Sinclair, J.A., 2012. Making voting easier, convenience voting in the 2008 Presidential election. *Political Research Quarterly*, 65(2), pp. 248–62.

Amnå, E. and Ekman, J., 2014. Standby citizens: Diverse faces of political passivity. *European Political Science Review*, 6(2), pp. 261–81.

Berinsky, A.J., 2005. The perverse consequences of electoral reform in the United States. *American Politics Research*, 33(4), pp. 471–91.

Blank, R.H. and Hines, S.M., 2001. *Biology and political science*. London: Routledge.

Bryngelson, A., 2009. Long-term sickness absence and social exclusion. *Scandinavian Journal of Public Health*, 37(8), pp. 839–45.

Burden, Barry C., Fletcher, J.M., Herd, P., Jones, B.M. and Moynihan D.P., 2017. How different forms of health matter to political participation. *The Journal of Politics*, 79(1), pp. 166–78.

Butler, D.M., 2014. *Representing the advantaged: How politicians reinforce inequality*. Cambridge: Cambridge University Press.

Chalmers, D.A., 2016. *Reforming democracies: Six facts about politics that require a new agenda*. New York: Columbia University Press.

Clarke, P.J., Ailshire, J.A., Nieuwenhuijsen, E.R. and de Kleijn – de Vrankrijker, M.W., 2011. Participation among adults with disability, the role of the urban environment. *Social Science and Medicine*, 72(10), pp. 1674–84.

Denny, K. and Doyle, O., 2007a. Analysing the relationship between voter turnout and health in Ireland. *Irish Medical Journal*, 100(8), pp. 56–8.

Denny, K. and Doyle, O., 2007b. 'Take up thy bed, and vote': Measuring the relationship between voting behavior and indicators of health. *European Journal of Public Health*, 17(4), pp. 400–1.

Enns, P.K. and Wlezien, C., 2011. Group opinion and the study of representation. In P.K. Enns and C. Wlezien, eds. *Who gets represented?* New York: Russell Sage Foundation, pp. 1–25.

Gastil, J., 2000. The political beliefs and orientations of people with disabilities. *Social Science Quarterly*, 81(2), pp. 588–603.

Gilens, M., 2012. *Affluence and influence: Economic inequality and political power in America*. Princeton: Princeton University Press.

Gollust, S.E. and Rahn, W., 2015. The bodies politic: Chronic health conditions and voter turnout in the 2008 election. *Journal of Health Politics, Policy and Law*, 40(6), pp. 1115–55.

Karlawish, J. and Bonnie, R.J., 2007. Voting by elderly persons with cognitive impairment: Lessons from other democratic nations. *McGeorge Law Review*, 38(4), pp. 880–916.

Karp, J.A. and Banducci, S.A., 2000. Going postal: How all-mail elections influence turnout. *Political Behavior*, 22(3), pp. 223–39.

Marmot, M., 2015. *The health gap: The challenge of an unequal world*. London: Bloomsbury.

Mattila, M., Lahtinen, H., Rapeli, L. and Ja Wass, H., 2016. Terveys ja poliittinen kiinnittyminen. In K. Grönlund and Wass, H., eds. *Poliittisen osallistumisen eriytyminen. Eduskuntavaalitutkimus 2015*. Helsinki: oikeusministeriö, pp. 415–34.

Mattila, M. and Papageorgiou, A., 2016. Disability, perceived discrimination and political participation. *International Political Science Review* (online first) DOI: 10.1177/0192512116655813.

Miller, P. and Powell, S., 2016. Overcoming voting obstacles: The use of convenience voting by voters with disabilities. *American Politics Research*, 44(1), pp. 28–55.

Norris, P., 2004. *Electoral engineering: Voting rules and political behaviour*. New York: Cambridge University Press.

Ojeda,C., 2015. Depression and political participation. *Social Science Quarterly*, 96(5), pp. 1226–43.

Pacheco, J. and Fletcher, J., 2015. Incorporating health into studies of political behavior: Evidence for turnout and partisanship. *Political Research Quarterly*, 68(1), 104–16.

Peterson, S.A., 1990. *Political behavior: Patterns in everyday life*. Newbury Park: Sage.

Priestley, M., Stickings, M., Loja, E., Grammenos, S., Lawson, A., Waddington, L. and Fridriksdottir, B., 2016. The political participation of disabled people in Europe: Rights, accessibility and activism. *Electoral Studies*, 42(2016), pp. 1–9.

Prince, M.J., 2014. Enabling the voter participation of Canadians with disabilities, reforming Canada's electoral systems. *Canadian Journal of Disability Studies*, 3(2), 95–120.

Reitan, T.C., 2003. Too sick to vote? Public health and voter turnout in Russia during the 1990s. *Communist and Post-Communist Studies*, 36(1), pp. 49–68.

Schur, L. and Adya, M., 2013., Sidelined or mainstreamed? Political participation and attitudes of people with disabilities in the United States. *Social Science Quarterly*, 94(3), pp. 811–39.

Schur, L.A. and Kruse, D.L., 2000. What determines voter turnout? Lessons from citizens with disabilities. *Social Science Quarterly*, 81(2), pp. 571–87.

Schur, L. and Kruse, D., 2014. Disability and election policies and practices. In B.C. Burden and C. Stewart III, eds. *The measure of American elections*. Cambridge: Cambridge University Press, pp. 188–222.

Schur, L., Kruse, D. and Blanck, P., 2013. *People with disabilities, sidelined or mainstreamed?* Cambridge: Cambridge University Press.

Shields, T.G., Schriner, K.F. and Schriner, K. 1998a. The disability voice in American politics: Political participation of people with disabilities in the 1994 election. *Journal of Disability Policy Studies*, 9(2), 33–52.

Schur, L., T. Shields, Kruse, D. and Schriner, K., 2002. Enabling democracy, disability and voter turnout. *Political Research Quarterly*, 55(1), pp. 167–90.

Schur, L., Adya, M. and Kruse, D., 2013. Disability, voter turnout, and voting difficulties in the 2012 elections. Report to Research Alliance for Accessible Voting and U.S. Election assistance Commission, Rutgers University, smlr.rutgers.edu/disability-and-voting-survey-report-2012-elections (accessed 22.5.2017).

Schur, L., Kruse, D. and Blanck, P., 2013. *People with disabilities, sidelined or mainstreamed?* Cambridge: Cambridge University Press.

Shields, T.G., Schriner, K.F. and Schriner, K. 1998b. Influences on the political participation of people with disabilities: The role of individual and elite factors in 1984 and 1986. *Journal of Disability Policy Studies*, 9(2), 77–91.

Söderlund, P. and Rapeli, L., 2015. In sickness and in health. *Politics and Life Sciences*, 34(1), pp. 28–43.

Söderlund, P. and Rapeli, L., 2015. Personal health and political participation. *Politics and Life, Sciences*, 34(1), pp. 28–43.

Sund, R., Lahtinen, H., Wass, H. and Mattila, M., 2017. How voter turnout varies between different chronic conditions? A population-based register study. *Journal of Epidemiology and Community Health*, 71(5), pp. 475–79.

Teorell, J., Torcal, M. and Montero, J.R., 2007. Political participation: Mapping the terrain. In van Deth, J., Montero, J.R. and Westholm, A., eds. *Citizenship and involvement in European democracies: A comparative perspective*. London: Routledge, pp. 384–414.

Tokaji, D.P. and Colker, R., 2007. Absentee voting by people with disabilities, promoting access and integrity. *McGeorge Law Review*, 38(4), pp. 1015–64.

Urbatsch, R., 2017. Influenza and voter turnout. *Scandinavian Political Studies*, 40(1), pp. 107–19.

Verba, S., Schlozman, K.L. and Brady, H.E., 1995. *Voice and equality: Civic voluntarism in American politics*. Cambridge, MA: Harvard University Press.

Ward, A., Baker, P.M. and Moon, N.W., 2009. Ensuring the enfranchisement of people with disabilities. *Journal of Disability Policy Studies*, 20(2), pp. 72–92.

Wass, H. and Blais, A., 2017. Turnout. In K. Arzhaimer, J. Evans and M. Lewis-Beck, eds. *SAGE handbook of electoral behaviour*. London: Sage, pp. 459–87.

4   Health and political orientations

Introduction

There are significant differences in political participation between groups of people in different health categories. Poor health is associated with lower turnout in elections, but the relationship between health and other forms of participation is much more complex, as demonstrated in the previous chapter. In this chapter, we investigate this observation more closely. Differences in political participation have traditionally been explained by political orientations, that is, the way people psychologically approach political phenomena. In this chapter, we analyze these psychological or attitudinal differences between people in good or poor health, as well as discuss whether these differences could offer an explanation for varying levels of political participation.

In their classic study on civic culture, Almond and Verba (1965, p. 12) defined political orientations as "attitudes toward the political system and its various parts, and attitudes toward the role of the self in the system". Thus, these orientations are kinds of psychological links attaching an individual to the world of politics. In political psychology, orientations are often seen in terms of individuals' psychological resources, which either hinder or promote political and civic participation. Among the most important of these orientations are an interest in politics, a sense of efficacy and political knowledge (Barrett, 2015, p. 176). Political scientists have also emphasized the role of two additional critical indicators of the overall support for an entire political system: trust in political institutions and citizens' satisfaction with the way that democracy works (Zmerli and Newton, 2008). Trust in political institutions and confidence in the functioning of democracy are both crucial for democratic stability and good governance. Next, these orientations, along with their relationship with health and disability, are analyzed. At the end of this chapter, we concentrate on a slightly different kind of orientation. To conclude this section, we study citizens' self-placements on the political left-right dimension and its associations with health.

The analyses presented in this chapter are mostly related to Hypotheses 1 and 3 presented in the theory chapter. The first hypothesis suggests that poor health decreases political engagement, while the third assumes the opposite. As there is only a limited amount of previous evidence for the connection between self-rated health (SRH) and psychological engagement, we are not able to make strong predictions about the outcomes of our analyses. However, some previous results show that political efficacy is lower among people with disabilities (Gastil, 2000; Schur, Shields and Schriner, 2003), which leads us to think that the first hypothesis is more likely to be supported. With the ideological left-right identification, a different conclusion could be true. Some previous studies, to be reviewed later in more detail, show that poor health is likely to be connected with leftist orientations, indicating that, at least to some extent, political choices by those with health problems may be guided by rational self-interest.

Interest, efficacy and satisfaction with democracy

We start the analysis with three variables: political interest, efficacy, and satisfaction with the way democracy functions today. These factors are all potential precursors of political action. Hence, they form possible mobilizing links between health and more tangible acts of political participation. Disabilities or problems with health may focus individuals' attention away from general societal concerns to more intimate issues of everyday life. This can lead to decreased levels in both interest in politics and political efficacy, i.e., the belief that one is able to have an effect on political matters. Decreased efficacy can, in turn, be negatively related to the way citizens feel about the functioning of democracy.

Figure 4.1 plots the relationship between personal health and the four measures of psychological political attachment: interest in politics, feelings of internal and external political efficacy, and satisfaction with the way democracy is currently functioning in Finland. Each of the four panels in the figure uses two measures of health: SRH and the extent to which respondents' personal everyday lives are hampered by a long-standing illness or disability. This bivariate analysis shows that those in good health are most likely to have higher levels of efficacy and interest than those in poorer health. They are also more likely to feel satisfied with the current state of democracy.

However, it is noteworthy that, in these descriptive results, the differences are rather small. This is especially the case with political interest, which was measured by asking the question 'How interested in politics are you?' (answer categories were 'very', 'somewhat', 'not much' and 'not at all'). People in excellent and good health do show more interest in politics, but the difference compared with those in poor health is not big. This is relevant, as interest is often considered an indicator of motivation and, as such, a major precursor to political participation (Russo and Stattin, 2016). We also know from previous research and the results presented in Chapter 3 of this book that there are participation differences between people with differing health statuses. This initial finding suggests that these inequalities in participation are probably not explained by differences in political interest.

The differences between health groups are somewhat bigger when we look at how highly people estimate their personal levels of political efficacy, which can be divided into external and internal components. External efficacy is a measure

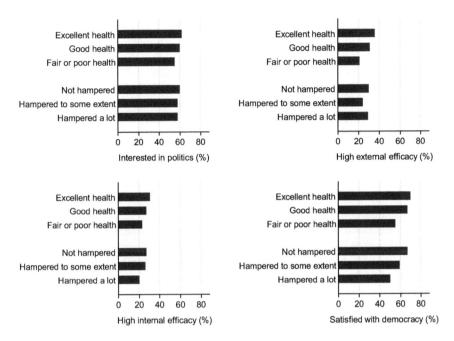

Figure 4.1 Health and political interest, efficacy and satisfaction with the way democracy works

of people's trust in the responsiveness of the political system to the interests of the citizens (Craig, Niemi and Silver, 1990). This was measured in the survey by responses to the statement 'I have no say on what the government or the parliament does' (response categories were 'agree completely', 'somewhat agree', 'somewhat disagree' and 'disagree completely'). The results show that those who report better SRH also evaluate the political system to be more responsive to their wishes, that is, they have higher levels of external efficacy. However, the results are rather more complicated, given that respondents whose lives are hampered a lot by long-standing illness or disability report as high a level of external efficacy as those whose lives are not hampered by health problems at all.

The differences are somewhat clearer in the case of internal efficacy, which is a measure of people's self-confidence in their own capability to understand politics (measured by posing the statement 'Sometimes, politics seems so complicated that I do not understand what is going on', again with four response categories) (see Niemi, Craig and Mattei, 1991). Here, respondents' better health is more systematically linked to a stronger self-assessed capability to understand and follow politics than in the case of external efficacy.

The attitude towards the functioning of democracy was evaluated with the question 'How satisfied are you in general with the way democracy works in Finland?' The respondents were offered four answer categories: 'very satisfied', 'fairly satisfied', 'somewhat dissatisfied' and 'not at all satisfied'. Disparities between health groups are markedly sharper when looking at this variable. Those with poor health or whose lives are hampered a lot by disabilities clearly report lower levels of satisfaction with the functioning of Finnish democracy.

As health is closely related to age and other background variables, the initial bivariate results presented in Table 4.1 are not enough to support strong conclusions on the relationship between health status or disability and political attachment. For this purpose, we need to use multivariate analysis, where we control for other potentially confounding factors. These results are shown in Table 4.1. For each item of attachment, we present two ordinal regression models. In the top part of the table, SRH is used as the main independent variable of focus, while the bottom part of the table repeats the same analyses but with the health variable measuring how much respondents' everyday lives are hampered by a disability or a long-standing illness.

As in the previous chapter, we present two models. The baseline model includes only health, gender, age and age squared (to take into account the possible curvilinear relationship between age and the attachment variables). Here, we can see the effect of health in its 'purest' form, without any intervening or confounding variables (see Chapter 2 for a more detailed discussion on the modelling strategy). The full model includes a more extensive set of control variables, such that this model enables us to evaluate how the inclusion of controls affect the initial relationship detected in the baseline model.[1] In order to save space, we do not report these coefficients in the tables.

The results in Table 4.1 present us with a more varied picture of the relationship between political orientations and health. First, when one compares the results between the baseline models and the full models, the relationship between health and attachment is stronger in the baseline models. This was expected as the relationships between health, demographic factors and socio-economic variables are very complicated and often reciprocal. Given this complexity, we should be careful when interpreting the results. Second, the interpretation is further complicated by the fact that, in some cases, the results in the top part (with SRH) and the bottom part of the table (with disability) diverge. Statistically significant results with SRH may not be significant when the disability measure is used. This is probably because the two health measures gauge, at least partly, different dimensions of health. Self-rated health, in addition to more serious and chronic illnesses, may also include more sporadic and/or acute conditions, which may get better over time, sometimes even rather quickly. Disabilities or long-term illnesses, possibly even dating from childhood or early adulthood, are more likely to indicate conditions with which individuals have come to learn to live with.

Satisfaction with the way that democracy works leads to most robust results in Table 4.1. Irrespective of the measure of health or model we use, the relationship between poor health and a lower appreciation of the actual performance of democracy is statistically significant. With the other measures of political attachment, the results are less conclusive. People in poor health seem to have lower levels of external efficacy and interest, but these observations are mostly noticeable only

Table 4.1 Health, interest in politics and political efficacy (respondents over 23 years)

	POLITICAL INTEREST		EXTERNAL EFFICACY		INTERNAL EFFICACY		SATISFACTION WITH DEMOCRACY	
	Baseline model	Full model	Baseline model	Full model	Baseline model	Full model	Baseline model	Full model
GOOD HEALTH	0.34**	0.29*	0.54**	0.47**	0.15	-0.02	0.58**	0.49**
	(0.12)	(0.14)	(0.13)	(0.15)	(0.12)	(0.13)	(0.13)	(0.15)
EXCELLENT HEALTH	0.53**	0.31	0.69**	0.48**	0.35**	0.05	0.90**	0.66**
	(0.14)	(0.16)	(0.15)	(0.17)	(0.16)	(0.18)	(0.17)	(0.18)
Age	0.04	0.04	-0.02*	-0.05*	-0.04	-0.05*	0.02	-0.01
	(0.04)	(0.02)	(0.02)	(0.02)	(0.02)	(0.02)	(0.02)	(0.03)
Age²	-0.00	-0.00	0.00	0.00	0.00	0.00*	-0.00	0.00
	(0.00)	(0.00)	(0.00)	(0.00)	(0.00)	(0.00)	(0.00)	(0.00)
Gender (female)	-0.35**	-0.43**	-0.04**	-0.16	-0.45**	-0.62**	-0.07	-0.04
	(0.10)	(0.11)	(0.09)	(0.11)	(0.10)	(0.11)	(0.11)	(0.13)
Observations	1,886	1,751	1,859	1,563	1,852	1,561	1,854	1,557

	POLITICAL INTEREST		EXTERNAL EFFICACY		INTERNAL EFFICACY		SATISFACTION WITH DEMOCRACY	
	Baseline model	Full model	Baseline model	Full model	Baseline model	Full model	Baseline model	Full model
HAMPERED A LOT	-0.07	0.04	-0.36	-0.17	-0.31	0.03	-0.96**	-1.08**
	(0.21)	(0.27)	(0.25)	(0.29)	(0.20)	(0.26)	(0.26)	(0.30)
HAMPERED A LITTLE	-0.11	-0.07	-0.30*	-0.23	0.05	0.16	-0.39**	-0.40**
	(0.12)	(0.13)	(0.12)	(0.14)	(0.14)	(0.15)	(0.13)	(0.14)
Age	0.04	0.05	-0.03	-0.06*	-0.04*	-0.05*	0.02	0.01
	(0.02)	(0.02)	(0.02)	(0.02)	(0.02)	(0.00)	(0.02)	(0.02)
Age²	-0.00	-0.00	0.00	0.00*	0.00*	0.00	-0.00	0.00
	(0.00)	(0.00)	(0.00)	(0.00)	(0.00)	(0.00)	(0.00)	(0.00)
Gender (female)	-0.35**	-0.42**	-0.02	-0.14	-0.44**	-0.63**	-0.04	-0.00
	(0.10)	(0.11)	(0.09)	(0.11)	(0.10)	(0.10)	(0.11)	(0.13)
Observations	1,889	1,577	1,862	1,564	1,854	1,561	1,857	1,558

Ordered logistic regression. Standard errors in parentheses. ** $p<0.01$, * $p<0.05$. The coefficients for the control variables in the full models are not reported in the table.

when SRH is used. So, we should treat these results as provisional: it is quite possible, perhaps even probable, that problems with health lead to a weaker belief in the responsiveness of the political system and the interest one has towards it. The least support in the analysis relates to the idea that poor health is linked with low internal efficacy. This association is weak in the baseline models and disappears completely when we control for demographic and socio-economic background factors.

Political trust and knowledge

Next, we turn to political trust and knowledge. Again, while these two variables relate to cognitive dimensions that are closely related to participation, they have a wider normative significance as well. Knowledge about politics is often considered to be a key factor in the involvement of ordinary people in the democratic process (for a more extensive discussion, see Rapeli, 2014). For example, one of the leading democracy theorists, Robert Dahl (2000, pp. 37–9), noted that a necessary level of enlightened understanding is a crucial requirement for the democratic process to function as desired. From an individual's point of view, a certain level of knowledge is required to be able to effectively take part in the political process and make reasonable choices in the electoral process.

Thus, it is no wonder that high levels of political knowledge are frequently linked to increased political and civic participation (Verba et al., 1995, p. 363), although the relationship between these two variables is likely to be reciprocal: knowledge about politics may mobilize citizens to participate, while, equally, active political participation can lead individuals to seek more information about concrete political issues, which, at the same time, expands their general knowledge of politics and other societal matters.

The relationship between political trust and participation may be more complex. One way to approach political trust is to understand it as a psychological relationship between citizens and the institutions of a political system. Individuals' levels of trust depend on "evaluations of whether or not political authorities and institutions are performing in accordance with the normative expectations held by the public" (Miller and Listhaug, 1990, p. 358). Previous studies have shown that high levels of political trust are associated positively with institutional participation and negatively with non-institutional forms of participation (Hooghe and Marien, 2013).

While the field of trust studies in political science has flourished during the past few decades, only a small number of studies exists, which concentrate on the relationship between political trust and health. Two studies have looked at personal health in conjunction with political trust in Sweden, finding that there is a positive association between trust and health (Lindström, 2011; Lindström and Mohseni, 2009). However, summarizing the literature on health and political trust is a risky venture because the number of empirical studies is so low. The existing studies nevertheless show that poor personal health and low political trust are linked, although the theoretical understanding behind this finding is largely lacking.

In this study, we have followed the usual approach for measuring political trust and operationalized it by using an additive index formed by six items, which measure trust in six important institutions of the political system. These institutions are the parliament, political parties, the government coalition, politicians, local government decision makers and public officials. The actual wording of the trust items was as follows: 'Please tell me, on a scale of 0–10, how much you personally trust each of the institutions I read out. 0 means you do not trust an institution at all, and 10 means you have an extremely high level of trust.' To calculate the index, all six items were summed together and then divided by six to preserve the original 0–10 scale. These items form a solid base for the trust variable, as they all load strongly on a single dimension, while Cronbach's α for the trust index is extremely high (0.93).

Respondents' levels of political knowledge were measured by asking three factual questions relating to political life in Finland. The first asked about which political party is the largest in the Finnish parliament at the moment. As the Finnish party system is rather fragmented, with four (relatively) large parliamentary parties (and eight parties altogether), this question was not as easy to answer as it might initially appear. The respondents were given four choices to choose from, with about 71 per cent answering correctly. In the second question, respondents were asked to identify the (then) current minister for social and health affairs (again, with four alternatives). This was a difficult question, as only 29 per cent chose the correct option. The third question asked about the number of MPs in *Eduskunta* (the Finnish parliament); 77 per cent of respondents were able to answer correctly. In the final combined knowledge variable, 18 per cent were able to correctly answer all three questions, while 14 per cent were unable to correctly answer any of them.

Figure 4.2 depicts the levels of average trust and knowledge among groups of people in different health categories. The upper part shows the findings relating to political trust. Here, the differences are relatively clear: the better their health or the less their everyday life is hampered by illness, the more people trust the political system. On the contrary, the differences in political knowledge are significantly less marked. For example, the average number of correct answers for those in excellent self-rated health is 1.7, while the corresponding value for those in poor health is 1.5, indicating that the differences are, at least in this bivariate analysis, small.

In Table 4.2, we present the results from the multivariate regression analyses involving demographic and socio-economic control variables. When we look at political trust, the findings previously obtained from the bivariate analysis are mostly confirmed. Even when respondents' age and gender are controlled for, there are differences in trust levels between those in poor and those in good or excellent health (baseline models). Although the differences are somewhat attenuated in full models when education and other socio-economic factors are taken into account, they are still visible and statistically significant. People experiencing health problems are more distrusting of political institutions than those in better health.

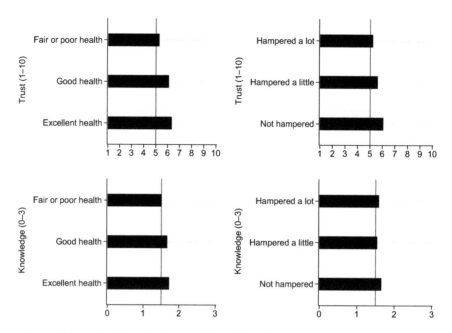

Figure 4.2 Health and political trust and knowledge (averages)

The situation is different for political knowledge. There are differences in the baseline models in the direction that was expected: citizens in poor health know less about politics than citizens with no health problems. What is important, however, is that these differences disappear when education and other socio-economic factors are taken into account (full models). This means that the health gap in knowledge vanishes, suggesting that the initially observed health differences in political knowledge are, to a great extent, explained by differences in respondents' social position. This means that, even if there are some disparities in political knowledge, these disparities are probably not caused by health differences as such, but by the fact that people with low education or otherwise in a lower social position are also more likely to be affected by health problems.

Left-right orientation

Next, we turn to the study of citizens' ideological identification. Results from the USA concerning the ideological leaning of people with disabilities are mixed. Gastil's (2000) study showed that people with disabilities are more likely to identify as Democrats, but this was not confirmed by later results by Schur and Adya (2013). When health is measured with the SRH indicator, the results are somewhat stronger. Subramanian and Perkins (2010) showed that identifying with the Republican Party was linked with better health in the USA, although a

Table 4.2 Health, trust in politics and political knowledge (respondents over 23 years)

| | POLITICAL TRUST | | POLITICAL KNOWLEDGE | |
	Baseline model	*Full model*	*Baseline model*	*Full model*
GOOD HEALTH	0.82**	0.57*	0.16**	0.08
	(0.13)	(0.14)	(0.06)	(0.06)
EXCELLENT	1.06**	0.70*	0.22**	0.04
HEALTH	(0.16)	(0.16)	(0.07)	(0.07)
Age	−0.02	−0.05*	0.02*	0.02
	(0.04)	(0.02)	(0.02)	(0.01)
Age^2	0.00	0.00	−0.00	−0.00
	(0.00)	(0.00)	(0.00)	(0.00)
Gender (female)	−0.02	−0.02	−0.19**	−0.19
	(0.10)	(0.10)	(0.04)	(0.05)
Observations	1,751	1,501	1,888	1,576

| | POLITICAL TRUST | | POLITICAL KNOWLEDGE | |
	Baseline model	*Full model*	*Baseline model*	*Full model*
HAMPERED	−0.86**	−0.75**	−0.07	−0.01
A LOT	(0.22)	(0.23)	(0.09)	(0.10)
HAMPERED	−0.46**	−0.38**	−0.12*	−0.07
A LITTLE	(0.14)	(0.14)	(0.06)	(0.06)
Age	−0.02	−0.05*	0.02**	−0.02*
	(0.02)	(0.02)	(0.01)	(0.01)
Age^2	0.00	0.00	−0.00	0.00
	(0.00)	(0.00)	(0.00)	(0.00)
Gender (female)	0.01	−0.00	−0.19**	−0.19**
	(0.10)	(0.10)	(0.05)	(0.05)
Observations	1,754	1,502	1,891	1,577

Ordinary least squares (OLS) regression. Standard errors in parentheses, ** $p < 0.01$, * $p < 0.05$. The coefficients for the control variables in the full models are not reported in the table.

more recent study indicated that, after controlling for socio-demographic characteristics, there were no mortality differences between Republicans and Democrats (Pabayo, Kawachi and Muennig, 2015). Outside the US context, studies have concentrated on analyzing the relationship between health and left-right orientation. These studies seem to confirm a linkage: poor health is related to increased support for the left in Europe (Subramanian, Huijts and Perkins, 2009) and Japan (Subramanian et al., 2010).

Figure 4.3 shows the bivariate relationship between SRH (top part of Figure), disability (bottom part of Figure) and the mean group positions on the left-right scale. In the survey, respondents were asked the following question: 'In politics, people often talk about the left and the right. Where would you locate yourself on a scale from 0 to 10 where 0 means the left and 10 the right?' As the bar chart shows, on average, people tended to position themselves a little to the right side of the scale midpoint. There are also some systematic differences between respondents

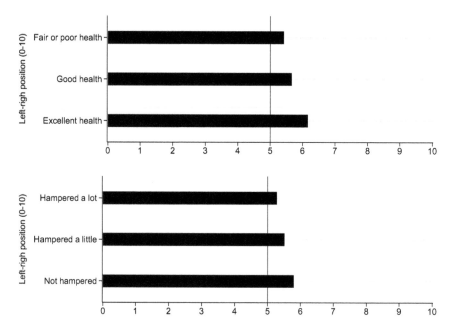

Figure 4.3 Average position on the left-right dimension

in different health groups: those in better health or without any life-hampering disabilities locate themselves more to the right than those with health concerns.

In Table 4.3, we analyze this association in more detail with linear ordinary least squares (OLS) regression. As before, we look at both the baseline model and the more extensive model with full controls. Regarding health, the results are statistically significant in both models and with both health variables. The effect is especially obvious in the extreme categories of the independent variables: those in excellent health lean most to the right, while those whose lives are hampered a great deal by long-standing illness or disability are most likely to identify themselves with the left. The difference is relatively small in size but consistent with the theoretical expectation.

With these data, it is impossible to offer a precise explanation for the association between health problems and leftist political self-identification. However, the observation is consistent with the self-interest hypothesis introduced in the theoretical section in Chapter 2. Problems with health are likely to make people more dependent on welfare services and financial support from the public sector. Thus, people in excellent or good health may feel less need to identify with leftist politics, as they are positioned more on the paying than the receiving side of public services. Similarly, those who actually use public health services may be more likely to support leftist parties, with a view to increasing the quality and quantity of public health services, or at least to fight possible cutbacks directed at these services.

Table 4.3 Health and left-right political position (respondents over 23 years)

	LEFT-RIGHT POSITION	
	Baseline model	Full model
GOOD HEALTH	0.24	0.17
	(0.14)	(0.15)
EXCELLENT HEALTH	0.74**	0.49**
	(0.16)	(0.17)
Age	0.04	0.02
	(0.02)	(0.00)
Age^2	−0.00	0.00
	(0.00)	(0.00)
Gender (female)	−0.13	−0.13
	(0.11)	(0.12)
Observations	1,810	1,538

	LEFT-RIGHT POSITION	
	Baseline model	Full model
HAMPERED A LOT	−0.52**	−0.49*
	(0.20)	(0.24)
HAMPERED A LITTLE	−0.28*	−0.14
	(0.13)	(0.13)
Age	0.03	0.01
	(0.02)	(0.03)
Age^2	−0.00	0.00
	(0.00)	(0.00)
Gender (female)	−0.10	−0.11
	(0.11)	(0.12)
Observations	1,813	1,539

OLS regression. Standard errors in parentheses ** $p < 0.01$, * $p < 0.05$. All control variables in the full models.

However, this 'political' interpretation may be too simple, at least on its own terms. It is also possible that an individual's left-right position is a marker of some specific latent attitudes, values or beliefs (Subramanian et al., 2009). For example, conservative values may be associated with health-promoting behaviours (such as eating, exercise or smoking habits or a willingness to seek medical help earlier). If this is the case, then the latent value (conservatism) would explain both a better health condition and a self-identification with the right. Thus, the association detected here and in other studies still requires more careful analysis to disentangle all the possible causal directions and linkages.

Conclusions

This chapter concentrated on citizens' psychological attachments to politics and how these attachments are connected to individuals' health status or disability. To some extent, the results were mixed and unable to offer a totally clear picture, although some significant patterns did emerge. If we look at the psychological resources, which are typically used to link individuals to the world of politics (i.e., political interest, efficacy, trust and knowledge), the main finding was either that those with good health had higher levels of these resources or that there were no differences between people under varying health conditions. In none of the factors examined here did respondents with poor health have higher levels than those in good health. In this sense, the results of this chapter give further support to our first main hypothesis: poor health decreases (psychological) political engagement.

Internal efficacy is a variable where no significant health effect was found, which indicates that people under different health conditions do not differ in terms of how they see their own ability to understand politics. The analysis of political knowledge indicated that, if there are health differences in knowledge, they are nevertheless small and can be explained by differing socio-economic situations between health groups. Together, these observations suggest that knowledge-based cognitive resources for political action do not explain the observed health-based differences in participation.

What about political interest and external efficacy? The results here were less straightforward. In analyses of SRH, some differences in interest emerged, but they were not replicated when the disability variable was used. Hence, we cannot say with much confidence that people in poor health are less interested in politics, although there were some indications that this might be the case, especially when looking at those with long-term illnesses. A similar pattern was noted with regard to external efficacy: there were some differences, but they were not large. People in good health were a little more willing to say that they have more influence on political decision makers, but the overall differences are small.

More consistent differences were found with regard to measures linked to the overall evaluation of how the political system works. First, health problems were connected to lower levels of political trust. People who have experience of poor health or disability tend to trust political institutions less than others. They are also less satisfied with the way Finnish democracy is currently functioning. Meanwhile, the analysis of left-right identification revealed significant differences: good health is associated with a more rightist self-placement and people with health problems are more likely to adopt more left-leaning positions.

In general, we can summarize the results in this chapter as follows. On the one hand, there is no or only a slight health gap in the way that individuals understand politics or have any factual knowledge of political matters. On the other hand, there are distinct differences in how people in good or poor health evaluate the functioning of the political system, indicated by the clear association between lower levels of trust and satisfaction and poor health or disability. Thus, to simplify: people with health problems are dissatisfied but not disengaged, at least not on the level of psychological attachment. This dissatisfaction may also partly explain their tendency to identify more with the political left.

Note

1 These variables are: age, age squared, married/living with a partner, education, income, life situation (full-time job, part-time job), unemployed, student, undergoing military or non-military service, pensioner, on parental leave or taking care of home), meeting friends, relatives or colleagues in non-work-related matters (several times a week, once a week, several times a month, once a month, less than once a month, never).

References

Almond, G.A. and Verba, S., 1965. *The civic culture*. Abridged version. Boston: Little, Brown and Company.

Barrett, M., 2015. An integrative model of political and civic participation: Linking the macro, social and psychological levels of explanation. In M. Barret and B. Zani, eds. *Political and civic engagement: Multidisciplinary perspectives*. Hove: Routledge. pp. 162–87.

Craig, S.C., Niemi, R.G. and Silver, G.E., 1990. Political efficacy and trust: A report on the NES pilot study items. *Political Behavior*, 12(3), pp. 289–314.

Dahl, R., 2000. *On democracy*. New Haven: Yale University Press.

Gastil, J., 2000. The political beliefs and orientations of people with disabilities. *Social Science Quarterly*, 81(2), pp. 588–603.

Hooghe, M. and Marien, S., 2013. A comparative analysis of the relation between political trust and forms of political participation in Europe. *European Societies*, 15(1), pp. 131–52.

Lindström, M., 2011. Social capital, political trust, and health locus of control: A population-based study. *Scandinavian Journal of Public Health*, 39(1), pp. 3–9.

Lindström, M. and Mohseni, M., 2009. Social capital, political trust and self-reported psychological health: A population-based study. *Social Science and Medicine*, 68(3), pp. 436–43.

Miller, A.H. and Listhaug, O., 1990. Political parties and confidence in government: A comparison of Norway, Sweden and the United States. *British Journal of Political Science*, 20(3), pp. 357–86.

Niemi, R., Craig, S.C. and Mattei, F., 1991. Measuring internal political efficacy in the 1988 national election study. *American Political Science Review*, 85(4), pp. 1407–13.

Pabayo, R., Kawachi, I. and Muennig, P., 2015. Political party affiliation, political ideology and mortality. *Journal of epidemiology and community health*, 69(5), pp. 423–31.

Rapeli, L., 2014. *The conception of citizen knowledge in democratic theory*. Basingstoke: Palgrave Macmillan.

Russo, S. and Stattin, H., 2016. Stability and change in youths? Political interest. *Social Indicators Research*, in press

Schur, L. and Adya, M., 2013. Sidelined or mainstreamed? Political participation and attitudes of people with disabilities in the United States. *Social Science Quarterly*, 94(3), pp. 811–39.

Schur, L., Shields, T. and Schriner, K., 2003. Can I make a difference? Efficacy, employment, and disability. *Political Psychology*, 24(1), pp. 119–49.

Subramanian, S.V., Hamano, T., Perkins, J.M., Koyabu, A. and Fujisawa, Y., 2010. Political ideology and health in Japan: A disaggregated analysis. *Journal of Epidemiology and Community Health*, 64(9), pp. 838–40.

Subramanian, S.V., Huijts, T. and Perkins, J.M., 2009. Association between political ideology and health in Europe. *European Journal of Public Health*, 19(5), pp. 455–7.

Subramanian, S.V. and Perkins, J.M., 2010. Are republicans healthier than democrats? *International Journal of Epidemiology*, 39(3), pp. 930–1.

Verba, S., Schlozman, K.L. and Brady H.E., 1995. *Voice and equality: Civic voluntarism in American politics*. Cambridge: Harvard University Press.

Zmerli, S. and Newton, K., 2008. Social trust and attitudes toward democracy. *Public Opinion Quarterly*, 72(4), pp. 706–24.

5 Health and the social context

Introduction

We are all affected by the social environment in which we live, including in terms of how we behave politically. Our social contacts and living conditions have an impact on the formation of our social identities, with everything adding up to affect how and why we engage in politics. In this chapter, we look at how the social context affects the relationship between health and political engagement. We examine two interconnected aspects of the social context, the social network and social identity, as possible mediating variables affecting how health and political engagement are connected.

The core idea that the social context affects how people behave politically is well established. According to Mutz (2002), social contacts are the most important mechanism for shaping individual political behaviour. According to Lyons (2011), at times, the influence of the social context over the political behaviour of the individual even overrides the impact of childhood political socialization. The mechanism through which the formidable force of the social environment primarily works is political discussion with other people (e.g., Klofstad, 2007). Even when discussions do not involve explicit attempts at political mobilization or to support a specific political candidate, informal discussion conveys both information and political preferences (e.g., Huckfeldt and Sprague, 1995; McClurg, 2003; Iglič and Font, 2007).

In addition to simply spreading information, contacts with family members, neighbours, colleagues and friends function as recruitment mechanisms, which mobilize people into carrying out political action (Iglič and Font, 2007, p. 188). Social relationships carry messages about what is considered desirable political behaviour, including non-participation. As McClurg (2003, p. 450) sums up, social networks lower the hurdles for participation by providing the individual with reasons to become engaged, as well as informational shortcuts needed to make political choices.

Social contexts also generate collective identities (Iglič and Font, 2007). A collective identity is "an individual's cognitive moral and emotional connection with a broader community, category, practice or institution. It is a perception of a shared status or relation, which may be imagined rather than experienced directly"

(Polletta and Jasper, 2001, p. 285). Collective identities have been particularly useful in explaining mobilization through social movements, which often seek to promote minority rights or raise awareness of a specific societal question. Collective identity theory has also been employed as a solution to the classic free-rider dilemma in collective action: why do some people choose to free-ride, while others become engaged? Whereas social networks provide a platform for *mobilization*, a sense of collective identity is therefore a potential source of *motivation* to engage. Moreover, as Eder (2009, p. 428) contends, by positioning the individual in relation to others, an identity helps people understand where they stand politically. Similar to social ties with other people, collective identities also work as a heuristic, making complex political choices simpler for the individual.

In this chapter, we test the idea that personal health and political engagement are affected by social networks and collective identities. We assume that social networks are an especially important channel for mobilization among people with health problems, which in turn constitute a collective identity that has consequences for political engagement. This is a fresh approach in the study of political engagement and health. Previous research has tended to exclusively focus on the resource theory for theoretical arguments. Whether discussing socio-economic or cognitive resources, poor health has been considered to be a condition that affects political engagement by making participation more arduous (see e.g., Pacheco and Fletcher, 2015, pp. 106–7). We suggest taking a different approach by examining the health–engagement relationship as a function of social networks. Instead of focusing on whether the individual possesses the time and money to become engaged, as analyses inspired by resource theory typically do, this chapter examines the role of social ties and identities as factors that may be particularly relevant in motivating and mobilizing people whose health puts them at a disadvantage.

Theoretical expectations

Although there is nothing new about using the social context as a predictor of political engagement, we argue that social context potentially has added significance in association with health problems. Anyone who suffers from a health problem is, in many ways, in a much more difficult position when it comes to taking part in societal affairs. There is an obvious risk that health problems lead to social isolation, given that poor health can make keeping in contact with other people more demanding. Preoccupation with health problems leaves less time and energy for social activities and may also cause a person to feel less eager to seek the company of others; not feeling well hardly makes anyone more sociable. If health problems require a lot of treatment or, for example, rehabilitation, there may not even be very much time for maintaining an active social schedule.

Mobilization, which primarily occurs through social networks such as voluntary organizations, the family and the workplace, makes politics more approachable in many ways. Talking about contemporary societal issues and a general sense of belonging within a certain social context provide cues and inspiration for political behaviour. Although a social network may also encourage disengaging from politics altogether, lacking a social network is a condition that most plausibly leads to political passivity. When nobody shows an interest in one's opinions and there is no outside pressure from other people to become activated, a person is certainly more likely to disengage from politics.

For reasons already stated, people with health problems seem to represent a particularly vulnerable group in this respect. Consequently, they also seem to be a group for whom social networks might be of particularly great significance in terms of mobilization. Findings concerning the social contacts and political engagement of other similarly disadvantaged groups, such as immigrants, also suggest that social ties are, in many ways, crucial in facilitating the political integration and mobilization of groupings, which run the risk of social isolation (e.g., Fong and Shen, 2016). As Ojeda (2015) has recently shown, social interaction plays a role in determining patterns of political participation among people suffering from depression. We therefore hypothesize that *social connections are more important determinants of political engagement among people with health problems than among people in good health* (H5). In other words, we assume that, while social connections are likely to have a positive impact on everyone's political engagement, they will be especially beneficial in facilitating engagement from people with health problems.

Collective identity adds another dimension to the broader question of how social environments affect political engagement. In a similar vein to social networks, people often share a sense of belonging with certain social groups whose members have something in common. The common denominator can be a number of things, such as ethnic background, social class or geographical area. Regardless of what it is, a collective identity often has consequences for how a person acts politically. Moreover, a sense of identity can be particularly significant in encouraging minorities or other potentially vulnerable groups to participate in political engagement (see e.g., Quintelier, 2009). Similar to social networks, collective identities provide a platform for political mobilization, but most importantly they should be seen as providing the motivation or incentive to engage in politics.

Health problems could plausibly constitute a characteristic around which collective identities develop. A health problem, which affects everyday life, is an important part of anyone's life experience and undoubtedly has an impact on a person's sense of identity and personality. Identifying with others who also suffer from health problems, or perhaps from the very same problem as oneself, may have a significant positive impact on political engagement. Given that collective identities are theorized to be a factor that increases motivation to become engaged, it seems reasonable to make a general assumption that *identifying with others who experience health problems increases political engagement among people with health problems* (H6).

As Polletta and Jasper (2001, p. 284) explain, a sense of identity also affects the forms of political engagement that people choose. If a person's motivation to engage in politics is based on a sense of specific identity, the choice of the mode of participation is likely to reflect the goal that the person concerned is seeking to achieve. A goal-oriented individual who is motivated by a health-related identity might be expected to choose particularly demanding, but also potentially productive, forms of political engagement, instead of forms that are easy and convenient, but hardly too effective. We therefore assume that *identifying with others who experience health problems increases the use of demanding forms of political engagement among people with health problems* (H7).

To distinguish between demanding and convenient forms of engagement, we follow the classification of different forms of political participation by Söderlund and Rapeli (2015, p. 32). They consider wearing a campaign badge, boycotting products and signing a petition as convenient forms of participation because "they pose fewer concrete obstacles", which might discourage or even hinder the engagement of people with health problems. We add contacting a politician or public official and expressing an opinion on social media to the list of convenient forms of participation in our empirical analysis. These are also considered convenient because they do not require a large investment in terms of time or money, or even a person to leave the confines of his home. We consequently consider party work and participation in voluntary organizations as demanding forms of participation. Moreover, a person who is or has been experiencing health problems could become active through patient organizations, which provide support for people with health issues or, for example, a certain illness or disability. In addition to voluntary organizations of any kind, we also look at patient organizations as one demanding, yet likely, form of political engagement among people with a health-based collective identity.

Analysis

As in the previous chapters, we use two measures of health: self-rated health (SRH) and disability, as well as include only respondents who are 23 years or older. To measure political engagement, we use different forms of political participation, political interest, and internal and external efficacy.

The analysis begins with a first look at how social networks and health-related social identity relate to the relationship between SRH/disability and political engagement without introducing control variables. We then proceed with multivariate regression analyses for a tougher test of the theoretical expectations.

Social networks, health and political engagement

We rely on two indicators for measuring the impact of social networks. To measure social activity, we use the question 'Compared with other people of your age, how often would you say you take part in social activities?', with the response being either 'much more seldom than most', 'more seldom than most', 'about the same', 'more often than most' or 'much more often than most'. The responses 'much more seldom than most' and 'more seldom than most' have been combined to form the 'socially passive' category, while the other responses make up the 'socially active' category. To measure social connectedness, we use the question 'How often do you meet socially with friends, relatives or work colleagues?', with

Table 5.1 SRH, social activeness and political engagement

%	Good health			Poor health		
	Socially active (n=1,037)	Socially passive (n=535)	Difference	Socially active (n=347)	Socially passive (n=428)	Difference
Voted	91.3	84.3	7***	83.6	81.5	2.1
Otherwise participated	81.9	68.8	13.1***	71.8	61.0	10.8**
Interested	66.2	53.8	12.4***	60.9	49.6	11.3**
Internally efficacious	32.6	21.0	11.6***	24.9	21.4	3.5
Externally efficacious	33.8	24.8	9***	22.7	18.9	3.8

Note: 'Voted' = proportion of respondents who said they voted in the latest Finnish parliamentary election. 'Otherwise participated' = proportion of respondents who said they had participated in at least one other way besides voting from a list of eight different participation forms. 'Interested' = proportion of respondents who said they were very or somewhat interested in politics. 'Internally efficacious' = proportion of respondents who either completely disagreed or partly disagreed with the statement, 'Sometimes politics seems so complicated that I can't really understand what is going on'. 'Externally efficacious' = proportion of respondents who either completely disagreed or partly disagreed with the statement, 'I have no say in what the government and parliament decide'.

the response being either 'several times a week', 'once a week', 'several times a month', 'once a month', 'less than once a month' or 'never'. Those who say they meet others once a month or less have been collapsed into the 'socially disconnected' group, while the rest are included in the 'socially connected' group. This approach aims at capturing two essential dimensions of a person's social environment: the extent to which a person has a social life, and the intensity of a person's contacts with others in crucially important social networks, including the family, the workplace and friends. Given the large number of variables involved in the analyses, the dichotomization of the variables serves the purpose of making the reporting and interpretation of the results less laborious.

Tables 5.1 to 5.4 offer a first glimpse at the hypothesis according to which social networks should be particularly important for engaging people with health problems. The tables only consider health, social activity/networks and political engagement without introducing any controls. If the hypothesis is supported, we should see particularly significant differences in political engagement among people in poor health, depending on whether they are socially active or passive.

As the theory of social context assumes, social activity seems to increase political engagement, but mostly among people in good health (Table 5.1). Among people with poor SRH, social activity is only positively and statistically significantly related to political interest and participation through other forms besides voting. But the corresponding difference is even larger among people in good health. In fact, the expected positive impact of social activity on political engagement is obvious and statistically significant on all counts for people in good health, but

Table 5.2 Disability, social activeness and political engagement

%	Not hampered by disability			Hampered by disability		
	Socially active (n=1,054)	Socially passive (n=601)	Difference	Socially active (n=335)	Socially passive (n=362)	Difference
Voted	89.9	82.7	7.2***	87.7	83.6	4.1+
Otherwise participated	78.9	63.1	15.8***	80.6	69.3	11.3***
Interested	65.7	50.1	15.6***	61.8	55.0	6.8**
Internally efficacious	30.6	22.1	8.5***	30.2	19.3	10.9***
Externally efficacious	31.8	24.8	7***	28.4	20.4	8**

Note: For the coding of political engagement variables, see 'NOTE' in Table 5.1.

not for people in poor health. Hypothesis 4 is therefore clearly not supported, as the results suggest that social activity has only a very limited bearing on those with poor health.

Switching SRH to disability changes the picture somewhat (Table 5.2). Although being socially active seems more important in terms of disability than SRH, social activity again plays a bigger role for people without a disability. The only situations where the hypothesis is (weakly) supported concern the impact of disability on internal and external efficacy. The gaps in efficacy between the socially active and the socially passive are slightly bigger among people who suffer from a disability.

In more general terms, the first two tables show that an active social life is conducive to all types of political engagement, thus lending support to the social context model of political behaviour. The differences between the socially active and the socially passive in many cases exceed 10 percentage points. The differences are particularly sizable when it comes to other forms of political participation besides voting, as well as for political interest. While political interest is essentially an indicator of motivation, political participation beyond voting also arguably signifies a high level of motivation. It therefore seems as if social activity could be more related to motivation, rather than mobilization, as our unsupported hypothesis assumed.

Let us continue testing the hypothesis in Tables 5.3 and 5.4 by looking at how the intensity of contacts with family and friends affects the relationship between health and political engagement.

Table 5.3 offers slightly more support to the hypothesis. Contacts with other people seem to matter more to people with poor SRH than people with good SRH. Social contacts are most important for political participation beyond voting among people with poor health, but there is also a noticeably similar difference for voting and external efficacy.

Table 5.3 SRH, social connections and political engagement

%	Good health			Poor health		
	Socially connected (n=1,377)	Socially disconnected (n=201)	Difference	Socially connected (n=609)	Socially disconnected (n=161)	Difference
Voted	88.9	91.5	−2.6	83.3	78.3	5.0[+]
Otherwise participated	78.1	73.6	4.5[+]	67.9	58.4	9.5**
Interested	62.0	63.2	−1.2	55.8	50.3	5.5
Internally efficacious	28.6	29.9	−1.3	23.0	22.0	1.0
Externally efficacious	31.6	24.5	7.1**	22.1	14.8	7.3**

Note: For the coding of political engagement variables, see 'NOTE' in Table 5.1.

Table 5.4 Disability, social connections and political engagement

%	Not hampered by disability			Hampered by disability		
	Socially connected (n=1,421)	Socially disconnected (n=226)	Difference	Socially connected (n=561)	Socially disconnected (n=136)	Difference
Voted	87.4	88.0	−0.6	86.5	81.6	4.9[+]
Otherwise participated	74.0	67.7	6.3**	77.1	65.0	12.1**
Interested	60.8	56.6	4.2	58.1	58.8	−0.7
Internally efficacious	28.4	23.2	5.2[+]	23.4	31.3	−7.9*
Externally efficacious	29.9	21.9	8.0**	25.8	17.7	8.1**

Note: For the coding of political engagement variables, see 'NOTE' in Table 5.1.

Table 5.4 reveals the same pattern in terms of disability, enabling a preliminary conclusion that contacts with other people are indeed more important in facilitating political participation among people with various health problems than people who are healthy. This effect, however, does not extend to other forms of political engagement and is admittedly modest in magnitude. It is nonetheless apparent that contacts with other people are more strongly and positively related to engagement than what we previously observed with social activity, which was measured as participation in various social events.

Let us now see whether these initial findings hold when several controls are introduced into multivariate regression models (Tables 5.5–5.8). Two types of

Table 5.5 SRH, social activity and political engagement: multivariate regression

	VOTING		OTHER PARTICIPATION		POLITICAL INTEREST		INTERNAL EFFICACY		EXTERNAL EFFICACY	
	Baseline model	Full model	Baseline model	Full model	Baseline model	Full model	Baseline model	Full model	Baseline model	Full model
EXCELLENT HEALTH	.900***	.632+	.045	-.278	.349**	.359	.246+	-.573+	.276*	-.110
GOOD HEALTH	.858***	.232	.071	-.039	.237*	.001	.114	-.313	.207+	-.008
Social activity	1.303***	.579	1.805***	1.561***	.989***	.852*	.851***	-.187	1.055***	.733+
Excellent health × social activity		.002		.228		-.346		1.362*		.406
Good health × social activity		1.230		.065		.420		.951+		.307
Age	.014	.041	.002	.026	.027+	.023	-.028	-.040+	-.026	-.028
Age²	.000	.000	.000	.000	.000	.000	.000	.001*	.000	.000
Gender (female)	.620***	.641***	.219**	.189	-.357***	-.389***	-.522***	-.730***	-.034	-.223*
Nagelkerke	.10	.16	.10	.17	.04	.10	.04	.12	.05	.09
Observations	1,894	1,598	1,898	1,602	1,896	1,602	1,863	1,585	1,872	1,588

Note: 'Fair' SRH and 'Poor' SRH have been combined to form the reference category. 'Social activity' = 'Compared with other people of your age, how often would you say you take part in social activities?', coded as follows: much less than most = 0; less than most = .25; about the same = .50; more than most = .75; much more than most = 1.

Table 5.6 Disability, social activity and political engagement: multivariate regression

	VOTING		OTHER PARTICIPATION		POLITICAL INTEREST		INTERNAL EFFICACY		EXTERNAL EFFICACY	
	Baseline model	Full model	Baseline model	Full model	Baseline model	Full model	Baseline model	Full model	Baseline model	Full model
NOT AT ALL HAMPERED	.020	.481	-.645**	-1.404***	-.208	-.580+	.327	-.162	-.317+	-.638+
A LITTLE HAMPERED	-.185	.232	-.304	-1.079*	-.236	-.385	.419+	-.027	-.499*	-.717+
Social activity	1.611***	1.924	1.993***	-.008	1.130***	.199	.907***	.268	1.159***	.851
Not at all hampered × social activity		-.862		1.882*		1.000		.393		.257
A little hampered × social activity		-.665		2.457*		.512		.581		.107
Age	.007	.038	-.002	.019	.023	.019	-.080+	-.040+	-.026	-.030
Age²	.000	.000	.000	.000+	.000	.000	.000	.001*	.000	.000
Gender (female)	.624***	.658***	.196*	.157	-.359***	-.392***	-.521***	-.730***	-.035	-.216*
Nagelkerke	.07	.14	.11	.19	.04	.10	.04	.12	.05	.10
Observations	1,894	1,598	1,898	1,602	1,896	1,602	1,863	1,585	1,872	1,588

Table 5.7 SRH, social connections and political engagement: multivariate regression

	VOTING		OTHER PARTICIPATION		POLITICAL INTEREST		INTERNAL EFFICACY		EXTERNAL EFFICACY	
	Baseline model	Full model	Baseline model	Full model	Baseline model	Full model	Baseline model	Full model	Baseline model	Full model
EXCELLENT HEALTH	1.140***	1.088	.297*	.787	.509***	1.088*	.360**	-.341	.414**	.571
GOOD HEALTH	.988***	.801	.258*	-.011	.338**	-.629+	.179	.468	.279*	-.396
Social connections	.312	.624	.542**	.756*	.345+	-.274	.100	-.330	.480*	.211
Excellent health × connections		-.468		-1.031		-.879		.336		-.443
Good health × connections		-.038		.163		1.186*		.276		.740
Age	.017	.047	.014	.037	.031*	.024	-.027	-.035	-.021	-.024
Age²	.000	.000	.000*	-.001*	.000	.000	.000	.000*	.000	.000
Gender (female)	.517***	.556***	.159	.154	-.415***	-.410***	-.549***	-.746***	-.082	-.258*
Nagelkerke	.08	.14	.06	.14	.03	.09	.03	.11	.04	.08
Observations	1,911	1,610	1,915	1,613	1,913	1,613	1,880	1,597	1,887	1,599

Table 5.8 Disability, social connections and political engagement: multivariate regression

	VOTING		OTHER PARTICIPATION		POLITICAL INTEREST		INTERNAL EFFICACY		EXTERNAL EFFICACY	
	Baseline model	Full model	Baseline model	Full model	Baseline model	Full model	Baseline model	Full model	Baseline model	Full model
NOT AT ALL HAMPERED	.215	.040	−.330+	−1.252***	−.070	−.585**	.389+	−.340	−.217	−.827**
A LITTLE HAMPERED	−.102	−.527	−.118	−1.149*	−.168	−.398	.433*	.054	−.440*	−1.864***
Social connections	.403	−.047	.604**	−.483	.387*	−.494+	.120	−.375	.509*	−.391
Not at all hampered × connections				2.075***		1.342***		.920**		1.034**
A little hampered × connections				1.422*		.290		.158		1.606*
Age	.014	.041	.011	.029	.028+	.014	−.029+	−.043*	−.021	−.032
Age²	.000	.000	.000*	.000*	.000	.000	.000	.001*	.000	.000
Gender (female)	.520***	.572***	.143	.126	−.414***	−.399***	−.546***	−.746***	−.085	−.261*
Nagelkerke	.04	.13	.06	.18	.02	.09	.03	.12	.04	.09
Observations	1,911	1,600	1,915	1,603	1,913	1,603	1,880	1,587	1,887	1,589

models are reported. The baseline models in the tables only include the coefficients for health, social network indicators, age, age squared and gender. In addition to these, the full model includes education, civil status, employment status and income. For more convenient reading, the tables only report the coefficients for the restricted set of variables, although more variables are present in the full model.

The tables report the results of logistic regression analyses. The statistical significance of the coefficients is based on the Wald statistic, which is not reported. The main focus in the results concerns the interaction terms between health and social activity/connections, which address the hypothesis by examining the gap in political engagement in relation to health and the social context. Regarding support for the hypothesis, we should expect negative coefficients for the interaction terms, indicating that political engagement is lower among the healthy and socially connected, compared with the unhealthy and socially connected.

Although the results show that SRH/disability and the social environment are, for the most part, statistically significant predictors of various forms of political engagement, they seldom involve the hypothesized interaction effect. But the two indicators of the social environment have a relatively strong and positive relationship with political engagement, as both theory and common sense would suggest; an active social life and contacts with family and friends generally speaking tend to increase engagement in politics. Typically, however, people are not differently affected by social networks depending on their health, as we assumed.

The only cases where our hypotheses receive support are those involving people whose daily lives are hampered by some disability in terms of other forms of participation besides voting and internal efficacy. For people with a disability of some degree, the social environment therefore seems disproportionately conducive to encouraging active political participation, as well as resulting in a stronger sense of self-efficacy within politics.

Collective identity, health and political engagement

Turning to collective identity, we examine the impact of the social environment on health from another point of view. We are interested in seeing whether identifying with people who suffer from health issues affects how health and political engagement are associated.

To study health-related collective identity, we first selected those respondents who reported that they were either currently suffering from a health problem, which affects their daily life, or suffered from such a condition previously in their life. Respondents who had never experienced a health problem that had limited their ability to lead a normal life were excluded from the analysis. In total, 964 respondents were included in the analysis.

To measure collective identity among the selected respondents, we use the question 'Do you feel solidarity with people who have a long-term illness or a mental health problem?', with the responses 'Yes, strongly' and 'Yes, to some extent' combined to form the group with a health-based identity (n = 1,441). Those who

Table 5.9 Health-related self-identity and political engagement: predicted probabilities

Predicted probabilities for:	Identifies with others experiencing health problems		
	Yes	*No*	*Difference*
Voting	87%	84%	3***
Political interest	61%	63%	−2*
Internal efficacy	24%	27%	−3***
External efficacy	23%	22%	−1*
Convenient forms of participation:			
Wearing a badge	15%	15%	0
Boycotting a product	33%	36%	−3*
Contacting a politician/official	21%	22%	−1
Signing a petition	40%	41%	−1
Expression of political opinion on social media	28%	33%	−5***
Demanding forms of participation:			
Working in a party	48%	50%	−2
Involvement with a patient organization	20%	16%	4***
Involvement in another organization	38%	37%	1

said 'No' formed the opposite group (n = 889). The original question was therefore recoded into a binary variable. The item is designed to tap the essence of collective identity, that is, the extent to which the respondent has a subjective sense of togetherness with others who share a similar condition, in this case, a health problem. We do not distinguish between SRH and disability in the subsequent analysis in order to keep the number of respondents in each respondent category large enough for robust analysis.

Table 5.9 reports the predicted probabilities for those with a health-based collective identity and those without with regard to the different forms of political engagement. We control for the same factors as in previous analyses, namely, age, age squared, gender, education, civil status, employment status and income. The last column in the table reports the difference in percentage points in the predicted probabilities for the two groups and whether the difference is statistically significant.

Hypothesis 6, which assumed that a health-based identity would lead to more political engagement, receives no support from our analysis. In fact, people who identify with others with a health problem are typically less politically engaged. Although the differences in predicted probabilities involve only a few percentage points, in many cases they are statistically significant. Only in the case of voting do we see the expected positive difference, which is hardly enough to salvage the hypothesis.

The results nevertheless lend some, albeit inconclusive, support for Hypothesis 7. Confirming our expectations, whether or not a person has a health-related collective identity is relevant in terms of becoming involved through a patient organization, i.e., an organization that seeks to promote the needs of people with a health problem. People with a health-based collective identity are much more active in such organizations, indicating support for the assumption that collective identity can lead to forms of political engagement that are more demanding and often time-consuming.

Regarding involvement in some other kind of voluntary organization or party work, we do not find evidence supporting our hypothesis. There is, in other words, no general pattern suggesting that self-identification would make people with health problems more likely to choose more challenging forms of participation than people without a similar self-identification. Participation through patient organizations stands out as the exception to the rule. There is nothing surprising about this finding, but it suggests that collective identity does provide a motivational base for engagement, which goes far beyond the most conventional mode of participation, that is, voting.

Conclusions

Although it would seem intuitive to think that social environments may have a significant impact on how people with health problems behave politically, our analysis suggests that there is only a limited effect. The results show that social networks have relevance as predictors of political engagement in general, but not especially for people with poor SRH or a disability. The impact of social networks is essentially the same, regardless of health status.

The expected interaction between the social context and poor health, however, was found in a couple of cases in our analysis of various forms of political engagement: political participation besides voting, and internal political efficacy among people suffering from a disability. For these forms of engagement, the social context played a more important role among people with health concerns than for people who reported being healthy. Social ties, then, seem particularly relevant in encouraging people to engage in politics beyond merely voting, with people whose lives are limited by a disability especially needing the encouragement to mobilize through other forms of political participation. The same positive effect of the social environment also seems to give people with a disability a sense of efficacy, or perhaps a political self-confidence. Considering that the measure of disability is aimed at capturing the *effects* of a disease or a physical limitation, rather than a more general feeling, as in the case of SRH, it seems understandable that disability, but not SRH, in combination with social connections, lends some support to our assumption. The more concretely a person feels the impact of a health problem, the more important is the social environment for political engagement.

Even if social ties do not help politically activate people with health issues, health-related social identities sometimes seem to do so. The finding that those who identify with others with a health problem are much more likely to participate in health-related voluntary organizations suggests that identity plays a role in shaping the political behaviour of people with health problems. The relationship could, of course, be reciprocal, such that participation in health-related associations also increases identification with other people experiencing health problems.

It is also worth noting that we find statistically significant linkages with regard to contacts with other people, rather than participation in various social activities. This finding significantly complements the widely accepted idea in the political participation literature that a person becomes attached to politics mainly through discussions involving family members, friends and colleagues. In our analysis, an active social life was not associated with political engagement as strongly as close human relationships.

Despite these findings, the more pressing question concerns why social connections and activities did not turn out to be as relevant for people with health problems in terms of political engagement as could reasonably be expected. While verifying the possibility that this could be a particularly Finnish phenomenon remains beyond our current scope, a few other explanations are worth speculating.

That said, it is important to note that the relative irrelevance of the social context for people with health problems is actually quite compatible with some recent findings produced by scholarship on political engagement. For instance, Klofstad and Bishin (2013) made a comparable discovery when looking at social connections and political engagement among immigrants in the US. Although drawing parallels between people with health issues and immigrants is not entirely unproblematic, the same theoretical expectations can be applied to both groups. As Klofstad and Bishin also argue (2013, pp. 296–8), becoming incorporated into society is especially important for the political mobilization of groups that do not have access to the level of political resources that would increase their ability and motivation to become engaged in politics.

There is also an entire body of literature and scholarly debate concerning how the prevalence of (dis)agreement in a person's social environment affects political engagement; some say that diverging political opinions diminish political engagement, while others insist that political diversity in fact invigorates people politically (see Nir, 2011, pp. 674–5, for a review). While this dimension was excluded from our analysis, it could affect the results as well, if the social contexts of people with health problems are, for some reason, predominantly conflicting or consensual. If the extent of disagreement or consensus is truly the driving force behind the impact of the social environment on political engagement, as many scholars seem to suggest, future analysis should take account of this shortcoming in our examination.

Leaving these more speculative explanations aside, the question as to why the social environment turned out to be mostly irrelevant in our analysis of health and political engagement still remains. Our analysis concerning health-related identity revealed that people with health problems who have a sense of health-based identity are also much more likely to engage in the activities of health-related voluntary organizations. This finding may also contain a clue to the modest impact of other social networks. It could be that the only mobilizing impact of any significance of the social environment on people with health problems comes from networks such as patient organizations, but not so much from other types of social environments. Perhaps, then, political mobilization among people with health concerns requires contact with others who are also affected by poor health. A related reason could be that, for people with health problems, the incentives to become politically engaged are very personal, making their motivation levels largely unaffected by social networks. For people who are affected by poor health, social networks involving family and friends could provide an important resource for help with daily tasks, but not so much a resource for political mobilization.

The results may also be seen as reassuring with regard to mainstream research on health and political engagement, which quite heavily relies on resource theory for theoretical inspiration. With only limited empirical relevance, the theories of social context and collective identity seem to be of secondary importance when it comes to determinants of political engagement among people with health problems. Although we should not completely dismiss the social context, the sources of mobilization and motivation for people in poor health to become politically active seem to lie, for the most part, outside their immediate social environments.

References

Eder, K., 2009. A theory of collective identity: Making sense of the debate on a 'European Identity'. *European Journal of Social Theory*, 12(4), pp. 427–47.

Fong, E. and Shen, J., 2016. Participation in voluntary associations and social contact of immigrants in Canada. *American Behavioral Scientist*, 60(5–6), pp. 617–36.

Huckfeldt, R. and Sprague, J., 1995. *Citizens, politics and social communication: Information and influence in an election campaign.* Cambridge: Cambridge University Press.

Iglič, H. and Font, J., 2007. Social networks. In J.W. van Deth, J.R. Montero and A. Westholm, eds. *Citizenship and involvement in European democracies: A comparative analysis.* London: Routledge, pp. 188–218.

Klofstad, C., 2007. Talk leads to recruitment – discussions about politics and current events increase civic participation. *Political Research Quarterly*, 60(2), pp. 180–91.

Klofstad, C. and Bishin, B., 2013. Do social ties encourage immigrant voters to participate in other campaign activities? *Social Science Quarterly*, 95(2), pp. 295–310.

Lyons, J., 2011. Where you live and who you know: Political environments, social pressures, and partisan stability. *American Politics Research*, 39(6), pp. 963–92.

McClurg, S.D., 2003. Social networks and political participation: The role of social interaction in explaining political participation. *Political Research Quarterly*, 56(4), pp. 449–64.

Mutz, D., 2002. The consequences of cross-cutting networks for political participation. *American Journal of Political Science*, 46(4), pp. 838–55.

Nir, L., 2011. Disagreement and opposition in social networks: Does disagreement discourage turnout? *Political Studies*, 59(3), pp. 674–92.

Ojeda, C., 2015. Depression and political participation. *Social Science Quarterly*, 96(5), pp. 1226–43.

Pacheco, J. and Fletcher, J., 2015. Incorporating health into studies of political behavior: Evidence for turnout and partisanship. *Political Research Quarterly*, 68(1), pp. 104–16.

Polletta, F. and Jasper, J.M., 2001. Collective identity and social movements. *Annual Review of Sociology*, 27, pp. 283–305.

Quintelier, E., 2009. The political participation of immigrant youth in Belgium. *Journal of Ethnic and Migration Studies*, 35(6), pp. 919–37.

Söderlund, P. and Rapeli, L., 2015. In sickness and in health: Personal health and political participation in the Nordic countries. *Politics and the Life Sciences*, 34(1), pp. 28–43.

6   Health and political participation from a cross-national perspective

Introduction

This chapter conducts a comparative study of health effects on political participation. We do not directly test any of the hypotheses proposed in Chapter 2, but rather introduce country context as a moderating variable in the relationship between health and participation. Even though we expect that poor health generally contributes to lower rates of political participation, the gaps between health groups are likely to vary across countries. In which countries are health gaps in political participation narrow and in which countries are they wide? Which contextual factors explain different health effects across countries? The latter question is particularly interesting as it is largely unknown which contexts are more conducive for political mobilization among individuals experiencing poor health, which, in turn, reduces the participation gap relative to healthy citizens.

We examine health gaps in political participation based on comparative survey data. First, different modes of participation (turnout, contacting a politician or government official, signing a petition and taking part in a lawful demonstration) are analyzed to identify patterns in terms of how participation gaps between citizens with poor and good health differ across countries. Second, the major aim is to explain the varying influence of health on turnout. We focus on the role of contextual factors, such as compulsory voting, type of electoral system, share of left-wing parties and trade union density.

Cross-national health gaps in political participation

Democracy is based on the principle of political equality. Citizens should have equal opportunities to express their views and participate in political and public life (Dahl, 1989, pp. 114–15). However, political equality is an ideal rather than a reality. Lijphart (1997, p. 1) observes that political participation is highly unequal and that "inequality of representation and influence are not randomly distributed but systematically biased in favour of more privileged citizens – those with higher incomes, greater wealth, and better education – and against less advantaged citizens." Some citizens have personal resources, motivation and access to recruitment networks, which foster political activity, as the *civic voluntarism* model proclaims (Verba et al., 1995). At the individual level, health is one of many factors that may, and does, contribute to disparities in political resources and action. However, it does not explain why the impact of health on political participation varies across countries.

Hence, the effect of health, or any other variable for that matter, on political participation is unlikely to be constant across different settings. We begin to describe how rates of political participation differ according to health status across a wide range of democracies. We mainly analyze survey data from seven rounds of the European Social Survey (ESS), collected between 2002/2003 and 2014/2015. One round of the World Values Survey is also used to describe health effects on voter turnout in other established democracies, such as the US.

Political participation is understood as "action by ordinary citizens directed towards influencing some political outcomes" (Brady, 1999, p. 737). Two modes of *conventional* political participation (Verba and Nie, 1972) are taken into account: turnout in elections and contact with a politician or a national or local government official in the last 12 months. Two modes of *unconventional* political participation (Barnes et al., 1979) form another group: signing a petition in the last 12 months and taking part in a lawful public demonstration in the last 12 months.

To quantify participation gaps between health groups, regression models are run separately for each country and political participation indicator. The regression coefficients will tell us, for each country, the strength of the effect of health on political participation. Political participation, coded 1 or 0, is the dependent variable. Health is measured with the same standard self-rated health (SRH) question as in the Finnish data, as we used earlier in this book: 'How is your health in general? Would you say it is very good, good, fair, bad or very bad?' Health is a continuous variable with five values, coded to vary between 0 (very bad) and 1 (very good). We control for age, age squared, gender and survey round. A linear probability model is applied by using the ordinary least squares (OLS) estimator (see Gallego, 2015, p. 31; Jusko and Shively, 2005). The regression coefficients and the confidence intervals produced by the multivariate regression models are extracted and stored. Interpreting the OLS coefficients is straightforward, since a coefficient of 0.10 suggests that the estimated turnout gap is 10 percentage points between a person with very bad health and one with very good health.

Estimations of health gaps in political participation

Health effects are most evident for voter turnout, according to the dot plots in Figure 6.1. The largest health gaps are found in Estonia and Switzerland. The coefficients 0.30 and 0.26 for the two countries reveal that the turnout gaps are 30 and 26 percentage points when going from very bad health to very good health. The health coefficient's mean is 0.14 for the 29 countries (SD = 0.06, min. = 0.00, max. = 0.30). The smallest health effects are found in Cyprus and Greece, where voting is compulsory by law. Electoral systems with compulsory voting are well

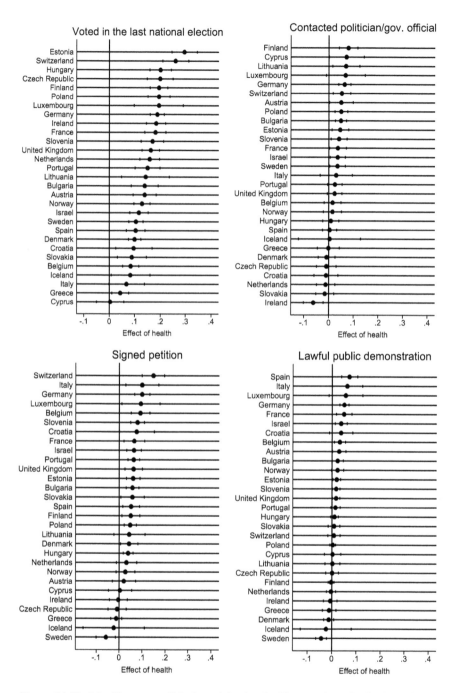

Figure 6.1 Health effects on political participation in 29 countries. The horizontal axis reports OLS coefficient estimates from within-country regressions of SRH on political participation. Bars denote 95 per cent confidence intervals

Source: European Social Survey (Rounds 1–7).

known to both raise and equalize turnout. For the two other compulsory voting systems in the sample, the effect of health on turnout is also small in Belgium, but larger in Luxembourg (even though the confidence interval is broad, indicating less precision in the estimate). It is noteworthy that neither Western European nor Eastern European countries form separate clusters. Instead, they are spread along the health effect scale.

The dot plots in Figure 6.2 are based on the sixth wave of the World Values Survey (2010–2014). Two questions were asked about electoral participation at the national and local levels: '*When elections take place, do you vote always, usually or never?*' Data for various established democracies are used to assess the health effects on turnout while controlling for age, age squared and gender. The health effects on voter turnout are most evident in the US, Estonia and Spain. As many political observers have pointed out, political participation is unequal in the US. The level of unequal participation in Estonia mirrors the finding above, based on the ESS. The two coefficients for Spain deviate (upwards) compared with the estimates above. The smallest turnout gaps are, in addition to Romania, found in Cyprus and Australia, which have compulsory voting laws.

Three dot plots in Figure 6.1 show the extent to which there are health gaps in other forms of political participation across countries. The frequency of participation

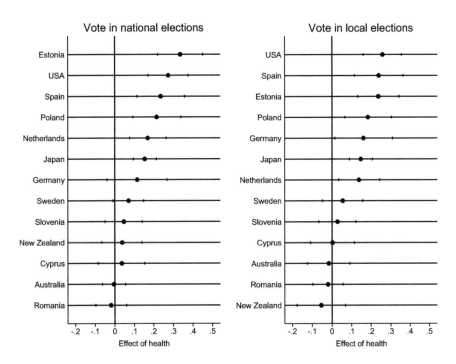

Figure 6.2 Health effects on self-reported propensity to vote in national and local elections in 13 countries. The horizontal axis reports OLS coefficient estimates from within-country regressions of SRH on political participation. Bars denote 95 per cent confidence intervals.

Source: World Values Survey (Wave 6)

is much lower for other political activities than voting. Among our indicators, signing a petition (22 per cent) is the most popular activity after voting, followed by contacting a politician or government official (14 per cent) and taking part in a lawful public demonstration (7 per cent). It is clear from the dot plots that the health effects are substantially smaller for alternative modes of political participation. The average health effects are 0.05, 0.03 and 0.02 points for the three non-voting forms of political participation. Furthermore, correlation tests affirm that the countries do not cluster in terms of the magnitude of health effects on different forms of political participation. Thus, for an individual country, the health effect on one form of political participation can be large, but small on another form of participation.

Theoretical predictions: context, health and turnout inequality

The previous section showed that there is substantial variation in turnout rates between voters with different health statuses, and much more so for turnout than other forms of political participation. It therefore makes sense to examine the cross-national variability in health effects on turnout. Our aim is to explain the turnout gaps between health groups by focusing on contextual features that may shape turnout inequality. We do *not* examine how health predicts low or high levels of voter turnout at the aggregate level. However, national turnout and turnout inequality are linked because group bias tends to increase as overall turnout decreases. Tingsten's (1937) 'law of dispersion' states that the differences in turnout rates between subgroups are smaller the higher overall turnout is. From a mathematical point of view, it is only logical that turnout gaps narrow as overall turnout approaches its maximum possible value (i.e., almost everybody turns out to vote).

Inequality in participation between more privileged and less advantaged citizens has been shown to be magnified in various institutional, political, economic and social environments. Studies in the past have focused on turnout gaps, for example, between generally disadvantaged and advantaged (Anduiza, 2002), politically interested and uninterested (Söderlund et al., 2011), less and more informed (Fischer et al., 2008; Jusko and Shively, 2005), less and more educated (Gallego, 2010, 2015) and low and high income groups (Anderson and Beramendi, 2012; Solt, 2008). Since health status creates disparity in political participation, it is relevant to ask in which countries those with poor health face fewer structural impediments. If the institutional or socio-economic setting is conducive to political participation for disadvantaged social groups, individuals with poor health participate in greater numbers, thus reducing the participation gap relative to those with good health. Small participation gaps imply that unhealthy and healthy citizens have more equal opportunities to participate, while advantaged and disadvantaged groups of voters are quite equally mobilized by different political parties and interest groups.

We focus on seven potential explanatory contextual factors, which may have a contingent effect on the relationship between health and turnout. First, the institution of *compulsory voting* compels people to vote, which should reduce turnout gaps. Second, *voting facilities* represent a group of institutional arrangements which make it more convenient for people to vote. Third and fourth, voting is arguably more complex in *candidate-centred systems* and party systems with a large *number of parties*, thus widening the turnout gap between disadvantaged and privileged social groups. Fifth and sixth, *share of left-wing parties* and *trade union density* should capture the positive effect of group-based political mobilization. Seventh, *economic inequality* is expected to exaggerate unequal turnout between low- and high-status groups.

Compulsory voting

Compulsory voting is an institutional mechanism that induces all social groups to vote, either because voting is a social norm or because they wish to avoid sanctions. Compulsory voting does, according to previous studies, effectively reduce the turnout gap between traditional low-participation and high-participation groups (Anduiza, 2002; Gallego, 2010; Lijphart, 1997). Four countries in our sample are coded as compulsory voting systems: Belgium, Cyprus, Greece and Luxembourg (Jensen and Spoon, 2011). While sanctions are imposed in three of the countries, penalties for failing to vote were removed in 2001 in Greece (but compulsory voting is still enshrined in the constitution).

Voting facilitation

Bias in turnout caused by unbalanced opportunities to participate can be narrowed by the implementation of different types of voter facilitation policies. In comparative investigations, however, the effectiveness of facilitation policies has been shown to be relatively modest (Anduiza, 2002; Franklin, 2002; Norris, 2004). When assessing the link between health and political action, institutional-level voting arrangements are particularly important since they may either enhance or hinder participation. In order to make voting more convenient, many countries have implemented various types of voter facilitation procedures, such as advance voting, absentee voting, assisted voting, proxy voting and mobile voting stations, which are specifically targeted for voting in hospitals and other institutions (Karlawish and Bonnie, 2007, p. 885). By reducing the costs of voting, such facilitation instruments are expected to increase not only participation, but also the socio-demographic representativeness of the electorate, evening up different sorts of bias in turnout (e.g., Berinsky, 2005, p. 471; Karp and Banducci, 2000, pp. 223–4; Tokaji and Colker, 2007, p. 1023). We therefore test if voter facilitation instruments are effective in reducing health-related inequalities in electoral participation. We use a facilitation index, which is a summary of six instruments: advance voting, weekend voting, number of election days, outside voting, proxy voting and postal voting (see Wass et al., 2017).

Party vs candidate-centred electoral systems

Turnout inequality between social groups will arguably increase as the costs of voting increase and as politicians' incentives to turn out the vote decrease (Kasara and Suryanarayan, 2015, p. 613). Preference voting has been demonstrated to discourage turnout among citizens with a lower education level or low levels of resources and motivation. In candidate-centred electoral systems with intra-party preference voting, voters must or may express preferences over candidates from the same party. Being confronted with many options, and having to choose between both party platforms and individual candidates, the voting procedure becomes more complex. For disadvantaged groups of voters, with fewer cognitive resources, collecting a greater amount of information to reach a decision raises the costs of participation (Anduiza, 2002; Gallego, 2010). The efforts in getting votes are less coordinated and efficient in candidate-centred systems, where individual candidates are more likely to run personal campaigns to target narrow constituencies (Söderlund, 2017). We expect that the turnout gaps are narrower in party-centred electoral systems and wider in candidate-centred electoral systems. Shugart's (2001) intra-party efficiency index arranges electoral systems on an ordinal scale, from party-centred to candidate-centred, according to the extent to which the electoral system provides incentives for individual candidates to cultivate personal, as opposed to party, votes (see also Söderlund, 2016).

Number of parties

The number of parties in a party system is another measure of the complexity of electoral choice. The broader the pool of electoral choices, the higher the cognitive and informational costs of voting. Proportional representation systems with large multi-member districts tend to produce a greater number of parties. Put another way, the number of parties in a party system is largely the product of the interaction between social heterogeneity and electoral permissiveness (Cox, 1997). Well-informed citizens are better able to deal with the complexity that a greater number of available alternatives bring. Less informed citizens are less likely to vote in political systems with many parties (Jusko and Shively, 2005). The level of turnout inequality should therefore increase with a larger pool of candidates to choose from (Gallego, 2010). We therefore test the hypothesis that the health gap in turnout gets wider when the political supply in a country's party system becomes more differentiated. The effective number of electoral parties, as measured by the Laakso-Taagepera index, is a standard measure to account for both the raw number of competing parties and the distribution of votes over those parties. Data were collected from Gallagher (2015).

Share of left-wing parties

Group-based political mobilization is expected to compensate for a lack of individual resources. Some parties are in a more advantageous position than others to muster the support of more disadvantaged groups in society, and vice versa. Left-wing parties in particular have been deemed as being more effective at mobilizing lower-status or resource-poor citizens. These parties compete on policy platforms favouring socially disadvantaged groups. Redistribution issues are also more likely to be politically salient in countries where left-wing parties are numerically strong (Gallego, 2010). People with poor health should have an incentive to participate if they are motivated to vote for a party that promises to deliver desired social and economic policies. We therefore test the theoretical prediction that, in countries where the share of left-wing parties is greater, citizens with poor health are to a greater extent mobilized, thus leading to smaller biases in electoral participation. Vote shares for social democratic, socialist, and communist parties are summed up. Data are mainly from the Comparative Political Data Set (Armingeon et al., 2016), but also from the Parliaments and Governments Database (ParlGov) (Döring and Manow, 2016).

Trade union density

The mobilization capacity of trade unions has also been acknowledged. This theory predicts that trade unions are able to enhance turnout among their members. In particular, the electoral mobilization of less educated working-class individuals could result in lower turnout inequalities (Gallego, 2010). The links between trade unions and political parties have weakened over recent decades. Trade union membership has also declined in many countries, particularly in post-communist countries, in tandem with weakening party identifications (van Biezen and Poguntke, 2014, pp. 210–11). Yet we expect that trade unions still have mobilization capacity, with turnout inequality expected to be lower in countries with higher trade union density. The variable measures net union membership as a proportion of wage and salary earners in employment (Visser, 2016).

Economic inequality

The final contextual variable is economic inequality, which refers to the dispersion of wealth within a society. In studies on the income effects on political engagement and participation, *resource theory* predicts that greater economic inequality results in "less political engagement among the relatively poor, but more political engagement among the better off" (Solt, 2008, p. 50). *Relative power theory* also predicts that economic inequality undermines political equality. People with lower relative incomes will be less politically engaged, since they feel their chances of influencing political outcomes are small, as opposed to rich individuals who have an influential position in the political arena (Goodin and Dryzek, 1980; Solt, 2008). A third theory, *conflict theory*, contends that economic equality should stimulate more interest and participation, regardless of an individual's income (Solt, 2008). We test the general claim that economic inequality depresses political participation, particularly among individuals in a disadvantaged social position (see also Anderson and Beramendi, 2012). In this case, the turnout gap between unhealthy and healthy citizens should increase along with greater economic inequality. Economic inequality is measured by using a Gini index of the distribution of net income (Solt, 2016).

Explanatory analysis of cross-national health gaps in turnout

We study inequality in political participation across 29 countries using seven rounds of the ESS (2002–2015). Countries that have participated in at least two rounds are included (except for Russia, Ukraine and Turkey). We use a two-step estimation strategy by first fitting separate regression models to survey data for several countries, then, in the second step, regressing the coefficient estimates on country-level predictors (Jusko and Shively, 2005). A two-step model is an alternative to multilevel modelling, where explanatory variables at different levels of analysis (e.g., individual and country level) are modelled simultaneously. However, running separate regressions for each country in a two-step manner is timewise and computationally more efficient than running multilevel logistic regression models with cross-level interaction variables.

The first step is identical to the procedure discussed earlier in the chapter: estimate the effect of health on turnout for each country separately and store the OLS regression coefficient. Even though voter turnout is a binary variable, a linear probability model is applied at the first stage by using the OLS estimator (see Jusko and Shively, 2005). OLS estimates have desirable properties of unbiasedness and efficiency. Surveys were pooled at the country level to identify the health effects for each country, rather than for each survey sample (the number of surveys per country varies between two and seven). The effect of health on political participation should not vary extensively over time within a country. In addition, the contextual variables are relatively stable over time. The dependent variable (coded 1 or 0) identifies whether or not the respondent voted in the last national parliamentary election. SRH varies between 0 and 1. Age, age squared, gender and survey round are controlled for.[1] Dummy variables for each survey round are included in order to control for possible temporal trends.

In the second step, we use the extracted coefficients from the first-stage models as the dependent variable and regress them on the country-level predictors to explain why the effect of health on turnout varies across countries. Since the surveys were pooled by country in the first stage, we calculate the means for each contextual variable for the period 2000 to 2014. With 29 countries involved, the number of observations for the second-stage models is small. Instead of running a multivariate regression model right away, we first present bivariate correlations between the health effects coefficient and each contextual variable (Table 6.1). In the first column, all countries are included in the calculation of the correlation coefficients. In the second column, the four compulsory voting systems are dropped to make sure that possible bivariate effects are not concealed by the strong turnout-increasing effect of compulsory voting.

Bivariate correlations

Table 6.1 shows that four of the seven variables have significant effects in the expected direction. First, the existence of compulsory voting laws decreases the gap in turnout between healthy citizens and citizens with health problems, as indicated by the negative coefficient. Second, turnout inequality between health groups is smaller in countries where left-wing parties are more dominant. Third, the greater the number of citizens who are organized in trade unions, the smaller the turnout gap. Fourth, the turnout gaps between citizens with poor and good health are larger in candidate-centred electoral systems than in party-centred systems.

With regard to the three other contextual variables, none of them is close to being deemed relevant in order to predict health gaps in turnout. In the case of voter facilitation instruments, we expected a negative correlation, but the positive correlation coefficient indicates that voter facilitation policies have not improved turnout equality (for a negligible effect, see Anduiza, 2002). It might well be the case that countries characterized by low or declining levels of turnout, as well as noticeable differences in participation between advantaged and disadvantaged groups in society, have been more motivated towards the introduction of various types of facilitation instruments (see Wass et al., 2017). Greater complexity in the form of a broader pool of party choices, measured by the effective number of electoral parties, does not seem to widen the turnout gap between health groups. Nor does economic inequality improve our understanding of why unhealthy individuals are less likely to vote than healthy individuals in some countries.

Table 6.1 Explaining health gaps in turnout: bivariate correlations

	All countries (N = 29)	Non-CV (N = 25)
Compulsory voting	−0.404*	–
Facilitation	0.312^	0.200
Candidate-centredness	0.319	0.760**
Effective number of parties	0.013	−0.063
Left-wing parties (%)	−0.452*	−0.405*
Trade union density	−0.443*	−0.449
Income inequality	0.031	0.110

Note: the table presents Pearson's correlation coefficients, as estimated in the second step of a two-step strategy. The dependent variable measures the health effect on turnout in each country, using a series of β estimates obtained in a first step where 29 country-by-country regression models were fitted. The first column includes all countries. The second column excludes countries with compulsory voting. ** $p < 0.01$, * $p < 0.05$; ^ $p < 0.10$.

Plotting contextual factors against health effects on turnout

Next, we examine the scatter plots for the four significant contextual factors. The estimated turnout gaps (and the confidence intervals) are plotted against each of the continuous contextual variables. It comes as no surprise that health gaps in turnout are smaller in compulsory voting systems (Figure 6.3). As discussed above, compulsory voting legislation, accompanied by sanctions, increases turnout and closes the turnout gap between socially privileged and disadvantaged citizens. While the health effect on turnout is non-existent or small in Cyprus (0.00), Greece (0.04) and Belgium (0.08), the coefficient is much larger for Luxembourg (0.19), although the confidence intervals are wide, suggesting imprecision. For the remaining graphs, only non-compulsory voting systems, shown as solid points, are included in the calculation of the regression lines. Compulsory voting systems are plotted, but shown as plus points (+) on the graphs.

The candidate-centredness of electoral systems, according to Shugart's (2001) index, appears to increase the turnout gap between individuals with different

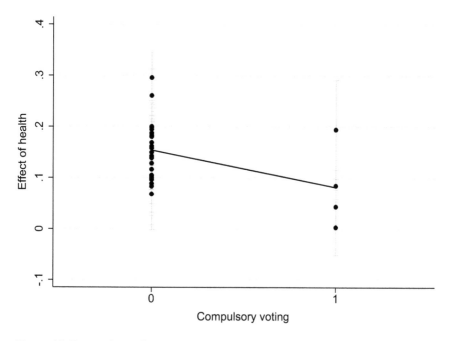

Figure 6.3 Turnout inequality and compulsory voting. The *y*-axis reports OLS coefficient estimates from within-country regressions of SRH on self-reported turnout. Bars denote 95 per cent confidence intervals. The *x*-axis reports whether or not compulsory voting laws are in place in a given country.

Sources: European Social Survey (Rounds 1–7); Jensen and Spoon (2011)

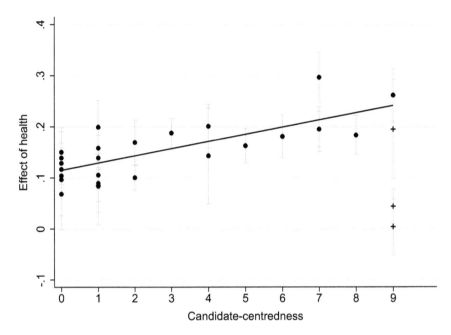

Figure 6.4 Turnout inequality and candidate-centredness. The *y*-axis reports OLS coefficient estimates from within-country regressions of SRH on self-reported turnout. Bars denote 95 per cent confidence intervals. The *x*-axis reports the candidate-centredness of electoral systems, i.e., the extent to which the electoral system provides incentives for individual candidates to cultivate personal, as opposed to party, votes. Non-compulsory voting systems, shown as solid points, are included in the calculation of the regression line. Compulsory voting systems are plotted, but shown as plus points (+).

Sources: European Social Survey (Rounds 1–7); Shugart (2001).

health statuses (Figure 6.4). Greater complexity and less coordinated mobilization efforts by parties and candidates at the district level were expected to discourage turnout. The most candidate-centred electoral systems are various open-list proportional representation systems (between 7 and 9 on the scale). They feature intra-party preference voting in different forms. At the other end of the scale (0 to 2), health effects on voter turnout are small in party-centred proportional representation systems (e.g., closed and ordered lists). As we move up the scale, we find mixed-member systems, plurality elections in single-member districts and majority elections in single-member districts.

Figure 6.5 reveals that, as the share of left-wing parties increases, the turnout gap decreases. This supports the assumption that socially disadvantaged citizens are, to a greater extent, mobilized in party systems where parties are generally supposed to be more effective at getting out the vote and attracting lower-status

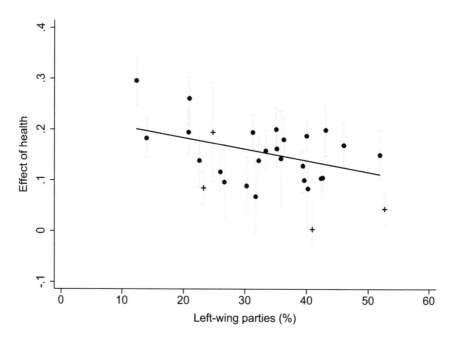

Figure 6.5 Turnout inequality and vote share of left-wing parties. The *y*-axis reports OLS
coefficient estimates from within-country regressions of SRH on self-reported
turnout. Bars denote 95 per cent confidence intervals. The *x*-axis reports the
share of the vote for left-wing parties, i.e., social democratic, socialist and
communist parties. Non-compulsory voting systems, shown as solid points, are
included in the calculation of the regression line. Compulsory voting systems
are plotted, but shown as plus points (+).

Sources: European Social Survey (Rounds 1–7); Comparative Political Data Set
(Armingeon et al., 2016); ParlGov (Döring and Manow, 2016)

or resource-poor citizens. However, four candidate-centred electoral systems with
larger turnout gaps (Switzerland, Ireland, Estonia and Poland) also happen to have
weak left-wing parties. Later, we need to run multivariate regression to examine
whether there are possible spurious relationships.

Trade union density was another proxy for group-based political mobilization. We do not claim that trade unions are particularly effective at mobilizing
less healthy citizens. A sounder interpretation is that the presence of strong trade
unions generally enhances turnout among their members. In Figure 6.6, the
majority of countries are located below the 40 per cent line in terms of trade union
density. Above this line, four of the five Nordic countries have small participation
gaps (while Belgium and Cyprus have compulsory voting laws and should be
disregarded when interpreting the regression line).

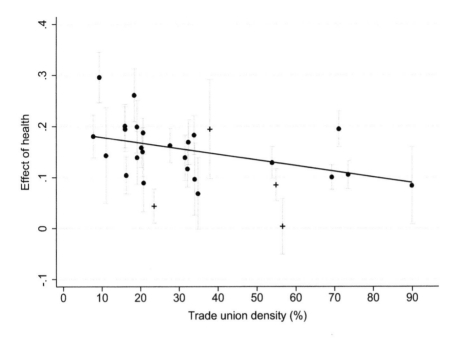

Figure 6.6 Turnout inequality and trade union density. The *y*-axis reports OLS coefficient estimates from within-country regressions of SRH on self-reported turnout. Bars denote 95 per cent confidence intervals. The *x*-axis reports trade union density, i.e., net union membership as a proportion of wage and salary earners in employment. Non-compulsory voting systems, shown as solid points, are included in the calculation of the regression line. Compulsory voting systems are plotted, but shown as plus points (+).

Sources: European Social Survey (Rounds 1–7); Visser (2016)

Multivariate regression

Finally, we test the explanatory power of the four contextual variables by means of multivariate regression (Table 6.2). We caution against over-interpreting the regression findings, given the limited number of observations. The independent variables are scaled to lie between 0 and 1, so as to ease the interpretation and comparison of the effects. Thus, the regression coefficient shows how much the turnout gap (i.e., the value of the health effect regression coefficient) increases or decreases when going from the minimum observed value to the maximum observed value. In the first model, OLS estimation with robust standard errors is performed. In the second model, we employ a feasible generalized least squares (FGLS) estimator. This procedure gives more weight to countries where the relevant regression coefficient in the first stage has been estimated relatively precisely (i.e., low standard errors), as suggested by Hanushek (1974) and Lewis and Linzer (2005).

Table 6.2 Explaining health gaps in turnout: multivariate regression

	OLS[1]	FGLS[2]
Compulsory voting (0/1)	−0.097*	−0.101**
	(0.034)	(0.033)
Candidate-centredness (0–1)	0.077 **	0.073**
	(0.026)	(0.026)
Left-wing parties (0–1)	−0.062	−0.061
	(0.038)	(0.037)
Trade union density (0–1)	−0.059 *	−0.058*
	(0.023)	(0.023)
Constant	0.179 **	0.181**
	(0.027)	(0.026)
Adjusted R^2	0.517	0.539
N	29	29

Note: Cell entries are regression coefficients (with standard errors in parentheses) in the second step of a two-step strategy. The dependent variable measures the health effect on turnout in each country, using a series of β estimates obtained in a first step where 29 country-by-country regression models were fitted. The contextual variables are rescaled to vary between 0 and 1, where 0 is the minimum observed value and 1 the maximum observed value. ** $p < 0.01$, * $p < 0.05$.

1 Ordinary least squares (OLS) with robust standard errors.
2 Feasible generalized least squares (FGLS) estimator.

The four variables jointly explain 50 per cent of the variation in the dependent variable. Compulsory voting and candidate-centredness are the strongest and most robust explanatory variables. Trade union density is a more modest predictor, yet statistically significant at the 95 per cent confidence level. However, as we observed above, the share of left-wing parties is not as strong or robust a predictor when controlling for other variables, particularly the candidate-centredness of electoral systems. Multicollinearity is of no concern, however, since the correlations between the contextual variables are low in magnitude.

Conclusions

In this chapter, we have demonstrated that health gaps in political participation differ in magnitude across countries. Cross-national differences in health-induced participation gaps were particularly evident for electoral participation. In countries such as Switzerland and Estonia, citizens with poor health are, relative to those with good health, much less likely to vote in elections. In other countries, however, being in a more difficult personal situation healthwise does not depress political participation as much.

Although poor health generally depresses political participation, we find some countries being closer to the ideal where people have equal opportunities in order to express their views and participate in political and public life. Some contexts are more conducive for political mobilization among individuals experiencing poor health, thus reducing the participation gap relative to healthy citizens. Four contextual factors appear to predict lower turnout gaps between health groups: compulsory voting, party-centred electoral systems, higher trade union density and a greater share of left-wing parties. Compulsory voting generally acts as a powerful institutional mechanism, which more or less forces everybody to vote, including citizens who are generally less likely to participate. Party-centred electoral systems are less complex, with fewer alternatives to consider, with parties assumed to be collectively more efficient in mobilizing voters than in candidate-centred systems. The importance of agents of mobilization was substantiated by the fact that turnout gaps were observed to be narrower in countries where trade union density is high. There were also indications that turnout gaps are smaller in countries where the share of left-wing parties is high, even though the findings were not as robust as for the other contextual variables.

Note

1   The number of control variables is minimized since we are interested in the impact of health on turnout. It is advisable not to control for variables, which are at least in part a consequence of the variable of interest (Gallego, 2010, p. 242). In the case of health, the direction of causality is not always clear, as discussed in Chapter 2. Hence, health is likely to be related to factors such as income, social status and social network position. Some might even argue that there is no causal effect of health on political participation, but rather that health is a proxy for other factors. As age and gender are not affected by health, they are used as controls.

References

Anderson, C.J. and Beramendi, P., 2012. Left parties, poor voters, and electoral participation in advanced industrial societies. *Comparative Political Studies*, 45(6), pp. 714–46.

Anduiza, E., 2002. Individual characteristics, institutional incentives and electoral abstention in Western Europe. *European Journal of Political Research*, 41(5), pp. 643–73.

Armingeon, K., Isler, C., Knöpfel, L., Weisstanner, D. and Engler, S., 2016. *Comparative political data set 1960–2014*. Bern: Institute of Political Science, University of Berne. [online] Available through: <www.cpds-data.org/> [Accessed 1 September 2016].

Barnes, S.H., Kaase, M., Allerbeck, K.R., Farah, B.G., Heunks, F.J., Inglehart, R.F., Jennings, M.K., Klingemann, H-D., Marsh, A. and Rosenmayr, L., 1979. *Political action: Mass participation in five western democracies*. London: Sage.

Berinsky, A.J., 2005. The perverse consequences of electoral reform in the United States. *American Politics Research*, 33(4), pp. 471–91.

van Biezen, I. and Poguntke, T., 2014. The decline of membership-based politics. *Party Politics*, 20(2), pp. 205–16.

Brady, H., 1999. Political participation. In J.P. Robinson, P.R Shaver and L.S. Wrightsman, eds., 1999. *Measures of political attitudes*. San Diego: Academic Press, pp. 737–801.

Cox, G.W., 1997. Making votes count: Strategic coordination in the world's electoral systems. New York: Cambridge University Press.

Dahl, R., 1989. *Democracy and its critics*. New Haven: Yale University Press.

Döring, H. and Manow, P., 2016. *Parliaments and governments database (ParlGov): Information on parties, elections and cabinets in modern democracies.* Development version [online] Available through: <www.cpds-data.org/> [Accessed 1 September 2016].

Fischer, S.D., Lessard-Philips, L., Hobolt, S.B. and Curtice, J., 2008. Disengaging voters: Do plurality systems discourage the less knowledgeable from voting. *Electoral Studies,* 27(1), pp. 89–104.

Franklin, M.N., 2002. The dynamics of electoral participation. In L. LeDuc, R.G. Niemi and P. Norris, eds. *Comparing democracies 2: New challenges in the study of elections and voting.* London: Sage, pp. 148–66.

Gallagher, M., 2015. *Election indices dataset* [online] Available through: <www.tcd.ie/Political_Science/staff/michael_gallagher/ElSystems/index.php> [Accessed 1 September 2016].

Gallego, A., 2010. Understanding unequal turnout: Education and voting in comparative perspective. *Electoral Studies,* 29(2), pp. 239–48.

Gallego, A., 2015. *Unequal political participation worldwide.* New York: Cambridge University Press.

Goodin, R. and Dryzek, J., 1980. Rational participation: The politics of relative power. *British Journal of Political Science,* 10(3), pp. 273–92.

Hanushek, E.A., 1974. Efficient estimators for regressing regression coefficients. *American Statistician,* 28(2), pp. 66–7.

Jensen, C.B. and Spoon, J.-J., 2011. Compelled without direction: Compulsory voting and party system spreading. *Electoral Studies,* 30(4), pp. 700–11.

Jusko, K.L. and Shively, W.P., 2005. Applying a two-step strategy to the analysis of cross-national public opinion data. *Political Analysis,* 13(4), pp. 327–44.

Karlawish, J. and Bonnie, R.J., 2007. Voting by elderly persons with cognitive impairment, lessons from other democratic nations. *McGeorge Law Review,* 38(4), pp. 880–916.

Karp, J.A. and Banducci, S.A., 2000. Going postal, how all-mail elections influence turnout. *Political Behavior,* 22(3), pp. 223–39.

Kasara, K. and Suryanarayan, P., 2015. When do the rich vote less than the poor and why? Explaining turnout inequality across the world. *American Journal of Political Science,* 59(3), pp. 613–27.

Lewis, J. and Linzer, D., 2005. Estimating regression models in which the dependent variable is based on estimates. *Political Analysis,* 13(4), pp. 345–64.

Lijphart, A., 1997. Unequal participation: Democracy's unresolved dilemma. *American Political Science Review,* 91(1), pp. 1–14.

Norris, P., 2004. *Electoral engineering: Voting rules and political behavior.* Cambridge: Cambridge University Press.

Shugart, M.S., 2001. Electoral "efficiency" and the move to mixed-member systems. *Electoral Studies,* 20(2), pp. 173–93.

Söderlund, P., 2016. Candidate-centred electoral systems and change in incumbent vote share: A cross-national and longitudinal analysis. *European Journal of Political Research,* 55(2), pp. 321–39.

Söderlund, P., 2017. Candidate-centred electoral systems and voter turnout. *West European Politics,* 40(3), 516–33.

Söderlund, P., Wass, H. and Blais, A., 2011. The impact of motivational and contextual factors on turnout in first-and second-order elections. *Electoral Studies,* 30(4), pp. 689–99.

Solt, F., 2008. Economic inequality and democratic political engagement. *American Journal of Political Science,* 52(1), pp. 48–60.

Solt, F., 2016. The standardized world income inequality database. *Social Science Quarterly*, 97. SWIID Version 5.1, July 2016 [online] Available through: <http://fsolt.org/swiid/> [Accessed 1 September 2016, checked 19 June 2017].

Tingsten, H., 1937. *Political behaviour: Studies in election statistics*. London: P.S. King & Son.

Tokaji, D.P. and Colker, R., 2007. Absentee voting by people with disabilities, promoting access and integrity. *McGeorge Law Review*, 38(4), pp. 1015–64.

Verba, S. and Nie, N.H., 1972. *Participation in America: Social equality and political democracy*. New York: Harper & Row.

Verba, S., Schlozman, K.L. and Brady, H., 1995. *Voice and equality: Civic voluntarism in American politics*. Cambridge: Cambridge University Press.

Visser, J., 2016. *ICTWSS data base: Version 5.1*. Amsterdam: Amsterdam Institute for Advanced Labour Studies (AIAS), University of Amsterdam. [online] Available through: <www.uva-aias.net/en/ictwss> [Accessed 1 September 2016, checked 19 June 2017].

Wass, H., Mattila, M., Rapeli, L. and Söderlund, P. (2017) Voting while ailing? The effect of voter facilitation instruments on health-related differences in turnout. *Journal of Elections, Public Opinion and Parties*, forthcoming.

7 Health and political representation

Introduction

In this book, we have thus far concentrated on the link between health and various dimensions of political engagement. While Chapters 3 to 5 dealt with the individual-level connections between health and political engagement, Chapter 6 provided a contextual analysis of the same relationship. Here, we shift the focus onto the consequences of health disparities for democratic outcomes by examining how different health groups are represented in democratic politics. We examine attitude congruence with health-related issues between citizens with various health statuses and both elected and non-elected candidates in the 2015 Finnish parliamentary elections.

Political citizenship has two core dimensions: the right to engage in politics (through civic, formal and non-parliamentary forms of political participation) and the right to exercise political power as a member of a body invested with political authority (e.g., parliament or local government) (Marshall, 1992/1950). Until this point, we have paid attention to the first dimension, i.e., the extent to which health influences the various forms of political engagement. In this chapter, the focus is set on the relationship between health and political representation: in other words, how well decision makers reflect the interests of different segments of society, including those groups that suffer from poor health or disabilities.

In line with the 'populist' view of democracy, governments should respond primarily or even exclusively to the policy preferences among citizens (Gilens and Page, 2014, p. 576; see also Pitkin, 1967, p. 61). Whereas descriptive representation refers to a resemblance of the composition of the representative body, and the electorate as a whole, substantive representation is more directly related to the correspondence between voters' preferences and MPs' actions. In this respect, the empirical evidence from the US context is rather disturbing, as the outputs of political decision making seem to better represent the interests of wealthier citizens (e.g., Butler, 2014; Enns and Wlezien, 2011; Gilens, 2012; for critics, see Bashir, 2015; Enns, 2015). This is partly related to the fact that these same groups are highly active politically (for a review, see Wass and Blais, 2017), meaning that their interests are more effectively promoted among decision makers through voting and other participatory channels. Besides the biased citizen input, the more

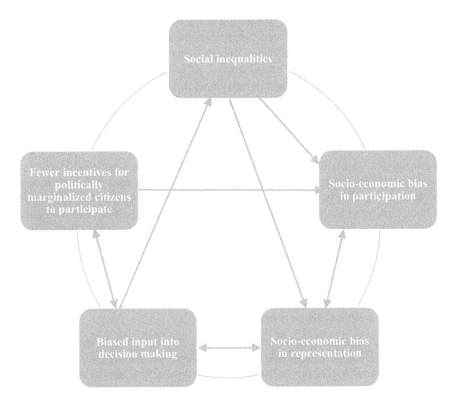

Figure 7.1 The elite cycle of political citizenship

privileged background of the legislators may contribute to the formation of an unrepresentative political agenda. This, in turn, may have a feedback effect on participation motivations among politically marginalized citizens. As a consequence, we end up with the elite cycle of political citizenship (Figure 7.1).

Pacheco and Fletcher (2015, 104) describe how such a situation would look in relation to health: "Compared to unhealthy, if healthy people are more likely to turn out and have systematically different policy preferences or predispositions, as we suggest, then electoral results and the policies that are enacted may have a 'health bias'. This suggests a feedback cycle linking population health to policies: increasing health disparities may produce increasing inequalities in policy representation, which in turn produces policies that may be detrimental to the unhealthy, which in turn creates even greater health disparities, and so on." Denny and Doyle (2007a) address the same issue while discussing the results of their empirical analysis: "Poor health leads to lower voter turnout, which suggests that the interests of the unhealthy are less likely to be represented in government. Unhealthy non-voters, therefore, represent an untapped source of electoral support. A political party which succeeds in attracting the unhealthy non-voters into the electorate by presenting a suitably targeted policy package, could help to minimize the inequality."

Here, we study the potential health bias by focusing on one particular dimension of substantive representation, i.e., opinion congruence between citizens and their representatives with health-related issues. Although there are several ways to conceptualize and operationalize it, which also affect the empirical results (Golder and Stramski, 2010), the idea of (ideological) congruence is rather simple. How distant from or proximate to the views of citizens are those of representatives on a particular issue? Admittedly, preferences and real-life decision-making situations are two separate issues due to institutional constraints, such as party discipline and social desirability bias (see von Schoultz and Wass, 2015, pp. 154–5). However, it seems plausible that the preferences of MPs might also manifest themselves at the level of behaviour (Esaiasson, 2000). The strength of this approach is that it enables us to detect (a) whether there are significant differences between various health groups and (b) whether healthier groups are better represented by the elected representatives and the candidates running for office. Before conducting an empirical analysis, we briefly discuss how health could influence political opinions and policy preferences.

Health and political preferences

As outlined in Chapter 2, health problems may increase an individual's (self-) interest in politics. When personal health is at stake, the payoff for a favourable policy outcome is high, even in the case of high costs. This logic stems from the expectation that changes in health cause shifts in policy preferences (Pacheco and Fletcher, 2015, p. 113). As more likely users of healthcare services, citizens suffering from ill health may be more inclined to support policies that aim to ensure public spending on social protection (Denny and Doyle, 2007b). This may also condition their evaluations on policy responsiveness. As demonstrated in Chapter 4, citizens who have experienced poor health or disability tend to trust political institutions less than others. They are also less satisfied with the way democracy is currently functioning.

However, self-interest might not be the sole reason for favouring a more substantial role for the public sector. The personal experience of health impairments or functional limitations can make a person sensitive not only to their own rights, but also to those of others, leading to an appreciation of equal opportunities (cf. Dalton and Welzel, 2014, p. 291), compassion and tolerance of social deviance, instead of emphasizing the responsibility of an individual and economic success (Gastil, 2000).

Empirical evidence in this field is scarce but provides some general guidelines. Robert and Booske (2011) noticed that those who rated their health as fair or poor were less likely to say that a person's health practices have a very strong effect on health. Correspondingly, compared with those with good or excellent health, they were more likely to recognize a role for the social determinants of health, such as access to affordable healthcare, health insurance coverage and income. In short, citizens without health problems perceived health more as a matter of an individual's personal choices, whereas those with health problems placed more emphasis on structural factors.

Meanwhile, Henderson and Hillygus (2011) noticed that health-related self-interest has an interesting conditioning effect on the relationship between partisanship and support for universal healthcare. Self-interest was operationalized with the question 'How much do you worry about facing major unexpected medical expenses?' The authors point out that, although not directly measuring insurance coverage, the question nonetheless captures a respondent's perception of his/her own interest in the policy proposal by combining it with personal concern about covering the costs of healthcare (ibid., p. 950). The results of the empirical analysis showed that those strongly committed Republicans who indicated worrying a lot about facing healthcare costs were in fact as likely to oppose universal healthcare coverage as most Democrats. In other words, personal health considerations modified the influence of partisan identity.

Disability has also been reported to influence policy preferences. In a telephone survey of New Mexicans with disabilities aged between 18 and 64 years, Gastil (2000) discovered that respondents with disabilities held more egalitarian attitudes and a greater interest in public healthcare than the entire study population. Correspondingly, Schur and Adya (2013), using nationally representative surveys, found that people with disabilities preferred a greater role for government in general. However, the preference for government responsibility in several areas, such as a guaranteed job for everyone who wants one and the provision of healthcare for the sick, did not extend to increased government spending. The authors suggest that, among other things, this may reflect a perception that government can exercise responsibility without spending more money through actions such as setting and enforcing rights and standards (ibid., p. 834). On the other hand, it is an illustrative example that citizens, regardless of their health status, often have incoherent policy preferences (for an in-depth discussion of the issue, see Achen and Bartels, 2016, pp. 30–6).

In line with these theoretical considerations and empirical observations, we expect that health differentiates policy preferences, i.e., those who suffer from ill health are more inclined to support greater governmental responsibility. Should that be the case, it is also likely that elected representatives and candidates running for office are, as a group, closer to healthier citizens who, on average, are more active voters, as was shown in Chapter 3. Another justification for this expectation relates to the social composition of the candidates. Although not directly measured, the above-average level of education and income among MPs and candidates running for office (Statistics Finland, 2015) suggests that their health status could also be better than the electorate as a whole. Furthermore, self-selection could play a role here, since campaigning and the actual work of an MP require good physical and mental condition.

Having said that, it is important to note that these expectations are made under admittedly simplistic assumptions. As people belong to several socio-economic categories and possess multiple identities, it is difficult to know in advance how particular individuals rank these in the level of self-conception and behaviour (see

Brown, 2006, p. 218). Moreover, even those who define themselves as members of a particular group may differ substantially in their political values and interests. Finally, representatives are also allegedly capable of representing the interests of anyone other than those of their own group (ibid.). It is, therefore, important to bear these caveats in mind when interpreting the results of our following empirical analysis.

Measuring opinion congruence

As already mentioned, congruence can be conceptualized and measured in several ways (Golder and Stramski, 2010, pp. 92–6). In the simplest manner, we can compare the absolute distance between one citizen and one representative. In practice, this is seldom meaningful, since one representative always represents several citizens. Hence, we can compare the congruence either between multiple citizens and one representative (e.g., median legislator) or between multiple citizens and multiple representatives. The latter many-to-many measure takes into account the distribution of preferences among the groups under comparison, instead of a simple mean or median position. It thus enables us to study how accurately a collective body of representatives reflects the ideological preferences of citizens (ibid., p. 95).

Using a measure that captures the deviations from the means is particularly important in the Finnish open-list proportional representation system with preferential voting, where policy differences occur not only between parties but also within. Karvonen (2014, p. 69) has a revealing description of the Finnish context in this respect: "It is not uncommon that the campaign of a, say, Left Alliance candidate appears much more left-wing-orientated than that of the party itself; and the same may go for Green, Conservative or Centre Party candidates"— considering that the entire distribution is particularly relevant in relation to 'valence' or consensual policy issues in which parties tend to agree on the ends of politics (for a review, see e.g., Green, 2007, p. 629), such as affordable healthcare. While discussing their empirical findings, Denny and Doyle (2007b) remark that if the main political parties do not differ enough in their policy positions on health, such that elections do not have consequences for the organization of health services, citizens with ill health may perceive the benefits of voting to be simply too low compared with the required effort to participate.

In the following analyses, many-to-many congruence is measured as the sum of absolute differences in cumulative functions of the two groups under comparison. Our preference distributions are discrete distributions with four ordinal categories (strongly disagree, disagree, agree, strongly agree). We first calculate the cumulative distributions of the (percentage) shares of the responses and then the absolute difference between the groups in each response category. Then, we sum these differences to an index, which describes the similarities in the distributions. If the responses are distributed equally, the index has a value of zero. In practice, the distributions are never similar: the larger the value of the index, the larger the differences. However, the problem with this measure is that it does not indicate the exact points where differences in preference distributions occur. To illustrate those, we also use simple cross-tabulations.

The analysis of congruence between various health groups and MPs/candidates running for office is conducted on the basis of five questions concerning health-care and social politics. These were presented to all candidates running for office in the 2015 Finnish parliamentary elections as part of the Voting Advice Applica-tion (for a review of Voting Advice Applications, see e.g., Fossen and Anderson, 2014) by Finland's national public service broadcasting company, YLE. After the elections, the responses by candidates were deposited in the Finnish Social Sci-ence Data Archive (FSD). We included the appropriate questions with exactly the same wording and response categories in our survey of the Finnish voting-age population and combined that data set with the one including candidates' responses (FSD3004). Altogether, our merged data set includes 1,783 voters, divided into three groups based on self-rated health (excellent, good and fair/ poor), while 1,998 candidates were divided into two groups (non-elected candi-dates and MPs). As in previous analyses, citizens' responses were weighted to match the entire electorate (see Chapter 2).

While YLE's Voting Advice Application included several questions, we included five that were directly related to social and health policy. These five questions relate to the following statements: (1) 'Finland should adopt a basic income to replace the current minimum level of social security'; (2) ' 'Finland cannot afford the current level of public social and healthcare services'; (3) 'Pub-lic authorities should get involved in the affairs of families with children more often'; (4) 'Social and healthcare services should primarily be provided by the public sector'; and (5) 'Senior citizens and their families should take more respon-sibility for the costs of elderly care'. For each statement, the possible responses were: (1) 'completely agree', (2) 'completely disagree', (3) 'partly disagree' and (4) 'completely disagree'.

Analysis

We begin reporting the results by looking at cross-tabulations of the responses to the health-related statements by survey respondents divided into groups by self-rated health and candidates in the 2015 Finnish parliamentary elections (Table 7.1). We have divided the candidates into those who did not get elected (n = 1,798) and those who were elected to the Finnish parliament (n = 200). For easier inter-pretation, we have collapsed the original four-step scale into two categories by combining the response options 'strongly agree' and 'agree' into 'agree', and 'strongly disagree' and 'disagree' into 'disagree'. Table 7.1 shows percentages of respondents and candidates who agreed and disagreed with the statements.

The first observation is that a variation in health-related attitudes is more evi-dent between citizens and candidates than between different health categories. Contradicting our initial expectation, differences in self-rated health do not seem to be very strongly connected to differences in attitudes. Only with regard to atti-tudes towards adopting a basic income, rather than the current system of social

Table 7.1 Agreement with health-related statements by respondents and parliamentary election candidates (% by column)

	Citizens by health			Candidates	
	Excellent	*Good*	*Fair/poor*	*Non-elected*	*Elected*
Finland should adopt a basic income					
Agree	60	66	73	69	54
Disagree	40	34	27	31	46
Finland cannot afford the current level of healthcare expenses					
Agree	50	48	47	31	27
Disagree	50	52	53	69	73
Authorities must intervene in the affairs of families with children					
Agree	78	77	76	17	10
Disagree	22	23	24	83	90
Healthcare services should primarily be provided by the public sector					
Agree	83	89	89	83	79
Disagree	17	11	11	17	21
Senior citizens and their families should pay more for elderly care					
Agree	29	27	28	17	14
Disagree	71	73	72	83	86

security, do we detect a significant variation between health groups: people in poor health are much more in favour of a basic income than people in good or excellent health. On other issues, the differences are quite modest, except perhaps for the opinion regarding whether healthcare services should primarily be provided by the public sector. As expected, people in poor health are more supportive of the idea, which is likely a reflection of their dependence on public healthcare.

However, much more differences in health-related attitudes can be detected between non-elected candidates and MPs. MPs are clearly less enthusiastic about a basic income than candidates who failed to become elected. While elected MPs' attitudes towards a basic income are fairly close to those of citizens with excellent health, they are quite distant from those who suffer health impairments.

Whereas about 50 per cent of all citizens across all health categories think that Finland cannot afford current levels of social and healthcare expenditures in the future, significantly fewer candidates and elected MPs feel the same way. Among MPs, only about one in four agreed with the statement. We see an identical pattern, although much stronger, with the next question. Over 75 per cent of respondents in all health categories agreed that public authorities should intervene more often in the affairs of families with children. Only 18 per cent of unelected candidates and about 10 per cent of MPs agreed with this, exposing a significant gap in attitudes between ordinary citizens and elected MPs. Survey respondents are also more in favour of making the elderly and their families pay more for elderly care than the candidates.

Yet, there is widespread consensus across all groups on the fundamental issue of whether healthcare services should be primarily provided as a public service with taxpayers' money. Almost 90 per cent of people in good or poor health consider healthcare to be a mainly public service, as do slightly over 80 per cent of people in excellent health. Among the elected MPs, this idea is supported by about 80 per cent, with a little more support among those who did not get elected. Overall, the rates are very high, suggesting that healthcare in the Finnish context is also a valence issue when it comes to the means by which to achieve the preferred end result. However, despite agreement on this particular issue, there are remarkable attitude differences between ordinary citizens and candidates running for office, particularly those who got elected.

To what extent are these differences in attitudes a cause for concern in terms of political representation? In Table 7.2, we complement the observations from cross-tabulations by calculating many-to-many congruence indicators between various health groups and non-elected candidates/MPs. In general, the results are in line with our expectations. On issues concerning the current level of health-care costs and the production of healthcare services by the public sector, both candidates and MPs are more aligned with healthier citizens. Voters with fair or poor health prefer the primary contribution to be made by the public sector and do not perceive the current healthcare costs to be too expensive. As indicated in Table 7.1, the differences between various health groups are rather small.

Perhaps the most noteworthy observation from Table 7.2 concerns the average rates of congruence for each health group, which show that citizens with fair or poor health are not as well represented as people in better health. They are, however, better represented by (i.e., they have higher congruence with) non-elected than elected candidates. This is particularly the case with attitudes towards a basic income, which is highly popular among citizens with poor health but supported to a lesser extent by MPs. Furthermore, in relation to the sustainability of healthcare costs and public sector responsibility for organizing health services, citizens who

Table 7.2 Many-to-many opinion congruence between candidates and health groups

	Non-elected candidates vs. health groups			Elected candidates vs. health groups		
	Excellent	*Good*	*Fair/poor*	*Excellent*	*Good*	*Fair/poor*
Adopt a basic income	28.5	19.8	11.2	20.3	35.2	53.6
Healthcare too expensive	42.5	39.7	36.6	37.7	34.7	35
Family interventions	123.2	119.9	122.4	132.2	128.7	131.2
Healthcare services	3.9	16	19.9	11.2	29.9	33.8
Expenses for elderly care	19.9	19.6	30.9	31.8	33.9	45.2
Mean congruence	43.6	43	44.2	46.6	52.5	59.8
Non-elected/ elected difference				−3	−9.5	−15.6

Note: The smaller the value of the many-to-many congruence indicator, the higher the congruence. See p. 106 for a description of the indicator.

suffer from ill health are closer to unsuccessful candidates. Hence, this situation is not as gloomy as the one suggested by Denny and Doyle (2007b) in relation to party positions in healthcare issues: at least on the level of individual candidates, there are options available.

The row indicating the difference in congruence between health groups and non-elected and elected representatives is strong evidence for the elite cycle of political citizenship framework, as presented in Figure 7.1. Arguably, the very essence of it is present: citizens with poor health have much lower congruence with elected candidates than non-elected candidates do with people in better health. As citizens with poor health have a lower propensity to participate, the candidates who better match their preferences are less likely to be elected, while those who do get elected produce unfavourable policies from the point of view of the less healthy. Admittedly, this is a rough generalization, but it nonetheless captures the basic dilemma.

Conclusions

Biases in political engagement and its unfavourable potential outcome, namely, unequal political representation, remain a puzzling issue. In spite of a myriad of analyses, it is still not fully understood why those groups that could benefit the most from political participation, such as the poor and the unemployed, have the lowest propensity to take part in political action. In Chapter 3, we showed that this is partly the case with citizens suffering from ill health or disabilities. Here, the aim was to examine the extent to which unequal health-related participation translates into unequal political representation.

The reason for unbalanced representative participation lies in the differences in preferences among those who participate and those who do not. In the case where the values and interests of non-voters differ from those of voters, citizens who cast their vote are substantially better represented (e.g., Teixeira, 1992, p. 102).[1] While several studies have reported no clear differences in the preferences of voters and non-voters, some biases have been detected (for reviews, see Gallego, 2015, pp. 172–4; Lutz and Marsh, 2007). Our analysis shows that preferences for five social and health policy issues do not remarkably differ among various health groups. The only noteworthy exception is a basic income, a social policy innovation in which one can detect a clear health gradient: the better the health condition, the lower the support for a basic income.

However, we also found some evidence that the preferences of healthier citizens are more aligned with non-elected candidates, and especially with MPs, than their less healthy counterparts. The implications of this finding are not straightforward. On the one hand, opinion congruence between citizens as a whole and MPs/candidates is relatively high with the issues covered here, except for governmental control over issues affecting families with children. This should be contrasted with the level of congruence with some other policy issues. Whereas studies on issue agreement have detected a high level of congruence between parties and voters with issues closely related to the left-right dimension (Costello et al., 2012), especially on issues that are salient to voters (e.g., Giger and Lefkofridi, 2014), noticeable discrepancies have also been observed concerning EU, immigration and foreign policy issues (e.g., Costello et al., 2012; Dalton, 1985; Holmberg, 2000, 2011; Mattila and Raunio, 2006, 2012; Lefkofridi and Horvath, 2012; Thomassen and Schmitt, 1999). On the other hand, the less healthy are, to a lesser extent, represented by unsuccessful candidates, and even more so by MPs. The fact that these two groups differ from each other suggests that the situation could be better, *provided that* citizens who suffer from poor health voted more actively and selected candidates on the basis of their preferences regarding health policy issues.

The situation in real life is obviously much more complicated. Lately, the entire idea of issue congruence has been revisited or even challenged (see Bühlmann and Fivaz, eds., 2016). Unlike the assumption made by the classical mandate model, representation is an ongoing interactive process, in which interests are reformed, strengthened and renewed at the level of both citizens and decision makers, rather than nailed down before the elections (Disch, 2016). In addition, it appears that policy preferences among political elites are structured differently than those of citizens, which makes it difficult for the former to accurately represent the latter (Rosset, Lutz and Kissau, 2016). Finally, even if issue congruence continues to matter as an indicator of representation, it is conditioned by issue saliency (Giger and Lefkofridi, 2016) and the voters' capacity to select parties and candidates that are closest to their own policy preferences (Lefevere et al., 2016).

With these caveats in mind, the results presented in this chapter should be considered as a cautious attempt to approach the complicated issue of political representation from the point of view of health. It is probably safe to say that health matters in terms of not only political engagement, but representation as well.

There may be multiple policy areas where it does make a difference, as suggested by the findings of Schur and Adya (2013) concerning people with disabilities. Health may also be an expanding field for 'representative claims' (Saward, 2010). With the ageing population, the saliency of health as a political issue is rapidly increasing. In the context of the Nordic welfare state, publicly financed health services continue to be a valence issue, as demonstrated here as well. This makes it difficult for political parties to characterize themselves as the owner of any particular health issue. As a consequence, it might be more difficult for voters who have a lower capacity to follow politics, due to health problems, to identify with those parties and candidates that would best match their own policy preferences.

Note

1   This argument is, however, problematic in a sense that non-voters could be indifferent to certain policy issues, which, in turn, lowers the desire to express an opinion and thus vote. Lijphart (1997, 4) points out that, once mobilized to vote, it is likely that previous non-voters would have rather different opinions compared with their responses in opinion polls.

References

Achen, C.H. and Bartels, L.M., 2016. *Democracy for realists: Why elections do not produce responsive governments?* Princeton: Princeton University Press.

Bashir, O.S., 2015. Testing inferences about American politics: A review of the "oligarchy result". *Research and Politics*, 2(4). Online.

Brown, M.B., 2006. Survey article: Citizen panels and the concept of representation. *Journal of Political Philosophy*, 14(2), pp. 203–25.

Bühlmann, M. and Fivaz, J. eds., 2016. *Political representation: Roles, representatives and the represented*. London and New York: Routledge.

Butler, D.M., 2014. *Representing the advantaged: How politicians reinforce inequality*. Cambridge: Cambridge University Press.

Costello, R., Thomassen, J. and Rosema, M., 2012. European Parliament elections and political representation: Policy congruence between voters and parties. *West European Politics*, 35(6), pp. 1226–48.

Dalton, R.J., 1985. Political parties and political representation: Party supporters and party elites in nine nations. *Comparative Political Studies*, 18(3), pp. 267–99.

Dalton, R.J. and Welzel, C., 2014. *The civic culture transformed*. New York: Cambridge University Press.

Denny, K. and Doyle, O., 2007a. Analysing the relationship between voter turnout and health in Ireland. *Irish Medical Journal*, 100(8), pp. 56–8.

Denny, K. and Doyle, O., 2007b. 'Take up thy bed, and vote': Measuring the relationship between voting behavior and indicators of health. *European Journal of Public Health*, 17(4), pp. 400–1.

Disch, L., 2016. Beyond representation. In M. Bühlmann and J. Fivaz, eds. *Political representation: Roles, representatives and the represented*. London and New York: Routledge, pp. 85–98.

Enns, P.K., 2015. Relative policy support and coincidental representation. *Perspectives on Politics*, 13(4), pp. 1053–64.

Enns, P.K. and Wlezien, C., 2011. Group opinion and the study of representation. In P.K. Enns and C. Wlezien, eds. *Who gets represented?* New York: Russell Sage Foundation, pp. 1–25.

Esaiasson, P., 2000. How members of Parliament define their task. In P. Esaiasson and K. Heidar, eds. *Beyond Westminster and Congress: The Nordic experience.* Columbus: The Ohio State University Press, pp. 51–82.

Fossen, T. and Anderson, J., 2014. What's the point of voting advice applications? Competing perspectives on democracy and citizenship. *Electoral Studies*, 36(2014), pp. 244–51.

Gallego, A., 2015. *Unequal political participation worldwide.* Cambridge: Cambridge University Press.

Gastil, J., 2000. The political beliefs and orientations of people with disabilities. *Social Science Quarterly*, 81(2), 588–603.

Giger, N. and Lefkofridi, Z., 2014. Salience-based congruence between parties and their voters: The Swiss case. *Swiss Political Science Review*, 20(2), pp. 287–304.

Giger, N. and Lefkofridi, Z., 2016. "Alignment of objectives" between parties and their electors: The role of personal issue salience in political representation. In M. Bühlmann and J. Fivaz, eds. *Political representation: Roles, representatives and the represented.* London and New York: Routledge, pp. 135–51.

Gilens, M., 2012. *Affluence and influence: Economic inequality and political power in America.* Princeton: Princeton University Press.

Gilens, M. and Page, B.I., 2014. Testing theories of American politics: Elites, interest groups, and average citizens. *Perspectives on Politics*, 12(3), pp. 564–81.

Golder, M. and Stramski, J., 2010. Ideological congruence and electoral institutions. *American Journal of Political Science*, 54(1), pp. 90–106.

Green, J., 2007. When voters and parties agree: Valence issues and party competition. *Political Studies* 55(3), pp. 629–55.

Holmberg, S., 2000. Issue Agreement. In Esaiasson, P. and Heidar, K., eds. *Beyond Westminster and Congress: The Nordic experience.* Columbus: Ohio State University Press, pp. 155–80.

Holmberg, S., 2011. Dynamic representation from above. In Rosema, M., Denters, B. and Aarts, K., eds. *How democracy works: Political representation and policy congruence in modern societies.* Amsterdam: Pallas Publications, Amsterdam University Press, pp. 53–76.

Henderson, M. and Hillygus, D.S., 2011. The dynamics of health care opinion, 2008–2010: Partisanship, self-interest, and racial resentment. *Journal of Health Politics, Policy and Law*, 36(6), pp. 945–60.

Karvonen, L., 2014. *Parties, governments and voters in Finland: Politics under fundamental societal transformation.* Colchester: ECPR Press.

Lefevere, J., Wahlgrave, S., Nuytemans, M. and Pepermans, K., 2016. Studying the voter-party match: Congruence and incongruence between voters and parties. In M. Bühlmann and J. Fivaz, eds. *Political representation: Roles, representatives and the represented.* London and New York: Routledge, pp. 152–69.

Lefkofridi, Z. and Horvath, K., 2012. Migration issues and representation in European liberal democracies. *Representation*, 48(1), 29–46.

Lijphart, A., 1997. Unequal participation: Democracy's unresolved dilemma. *American Political Science Review*, 91(1), pp. 1–14.

Lutz, G. and Marsh, M., 2007. Introduction: Consequences of low turnout. *Electoral Studies*, 26(3), 539–47.

Marshall, T.H. and Bottomore, T., 1992. *Citizenship and social class*. London: Pluto Press.

Mattila, M. and Raunio, T., 2006. Cautious voters – supportive parties: Opinion congruence between voters and parties on the EU dimension. *European Union Politics*, 7(4), pp. 427–49.

Mattila, M. and Raunio, T., 2012. Drifting further apart: National parties and their electorates on the EU dimension. *West European Politics*, 35(3), pp. 589–606.

Pacheco, J. and Fletcher, J., 2015. Incorporating health into studies of political behavior: Evidence for turnout and partisanship. *Political Research Quarterly*, 68(1), 104–16.

Pitkin, H.F., 1967. *The concept of representation*. Berkeley: University of California Press.

Robert, S. and Booske, B.C., 2011. US opinions on health determinants and social policy as health policy. *American Journal of Public Health*, 101(9), 1655–63.

Rosset, J., Lutz, G. and Kissau, K., 2016. Representation of political opinions: Is the structuring pattern of policy preferences the same for citizens and elites? In M. Bühlmann and J. Fivaz, eds. *Political representation: Roles, representatives and the represented*. London and New York: Routledge, pp. 117–34.

Saward, M., 2010. *Representative claim*. Oxford and New York: Oxford University Press.

Schur, L. and Adya, M., 2013. Sidelined or mainstreamed? Political participation and attitudes of people with disabilities in the United States. *Social Science Quarterly*, 94(3), 811–39.

Statistics Finland., 2015. *Background analysis of candidates and elected MPs in the parliamentary elections 2015*, Available through: <http://tilastokeskus.fi/til/evaa/2015/evaa_2015_2015-04-30_kat_001_en.html> [Accessed February 28 2017].

Teixeira, R.A., 1992. *The disappearing American voter*. Washington, DC: The Brookings Institution.

Thomassen, J. and Schmitt, H., 1999. Issue congruence. In Schmitt, H. and Thomassen, J., eds. *Political representation and legitimacy in the European Union*. Oxford: Oxford University Press, pp. 186–208.

von Schoultz, Å. and Wass, H., 2015. Beating issue agreement: Congruence in the representational preferences of candidates and voters. *Parliamentary Affairs*, 69(1), pp. 136–58.

Wass, H. and Blais, A., 2017. Turnout. In K. Arzhaimer, J. Evans and M. Lewis-Beck, eds. *SAGE Handbook of electoral behaviour*. London: Sage, pp. 459–87.

8   Conclusions

The overarching question in this book concerns when and how health is connected to the way in which people think about and participate in politics. As theoretical and conceptual relations between health and politics are complicated, and may take many forms, it should come as no surprise that our results failed to provide a simple, unambiguous answer to our question. Yes, health affects political engagement in various ways, but we must almost always qualify the answer somehow. For example, in some cases, good health fosters political participation, but the relationship is non-existent or even reversed in some other forms of participation.

In this concluding chapter, we review our results and discuss their importance in wider theoretical and societal contexts. We begin this section by summarizing our main empirical findings. After that, we discuss the implications of our results for the theoretical expectations that we presented as our main hypotheses in Chapter 2. We also readily acknowledge that our study is limited in many ways. Nevertheless, our results indicate some fruitful avenues for further research, which we discuss at this point. Finally, we offer some more normative ideas based on our research, especially with regard to how health differences are related to the discussion on inequality and inclusive democracy.

Summary of the main findings

Table 8.1 provides a concise summary of our main empirical results. While we have tried to crystallize the essence of the results into a few sentences in the table, the entirety of our findings is, of course, more complicated and nuanced. With the exception of Chapter 6, our results reflect the situation in Finland. However, most of our results, when comparisons are possible, are quite similar to those obtained in many countries. This gives us some confidence to claim that our results, concerning aspects that have not been studied elsewhere, can probably be generalized to wider contexts outside Finland as well. However, we also acknowledge the uncertainty related to this claim and encourage researchers in other countries to tackle similar questions within their unique contexts and data sets.

In Chapter 3, the focus was on the health gap in various forms of political participation. The empirical results showed that, in general, poor health depresses political participation, although there were some significant deviations from this

Table 8.1 Summary of main empirical findings

Chapter 3: Health and political participation	Although there are significant deviations from the pattern, poor health more often depresses political participation than mobilizes potential participants into action. On the other hand, those suffering from a long-term illness or disability were more active than their healthy counterparts on many counts.
Chapter 4: Health and political orientations	Poor health decreases political trust and external efficacy, but not internal efficacy or political knowledge to any marked extent. People with poor health identify more easily with the political left than people in good or excellent health.
Chapter 5: Health and the social context	Social networks have relevance as predictors of political engagement in general, but there is not so much difference in the effect between people with poor and good health. Those who identify with others with a health problem are more likely to participate in health-related voluntary organizations.
Chapter 6: Health and participation from a cross-national perspective	Health gaps in political participation differ in magnitude across countries. Cross-national differences in health-induced participation gaps were particularly evident for electoral participation. Four contextual factors appear to predict lower turnout gaps between health groups: compulsory voting, party-centred electoral systems, higher trade union density and a greater share of left-wing parties.
Chapter 7: Health and political representation	Preferences of healthier citizens are more aligned with non-elected candidates, and especially with MPs, than their less healthy counterparts.

pattern, especially when looking at people with disabilities or long-term illnesses. People who are not hampered in their daily lives by a disability show the lowest rates of political participation on most other counts besides voting, where differences are insignificant. Additionally, citizens who are most hampered by a disability are most active in terms of contacting a politician or a public official and signing petitions. This means that the effect of health on participation depends, first, on the type of 'health' that we are measuring and, second, on the type of political activity that we are looking at.

The analyses in Chapter 3 also addressed the question about whether health problems affect participation more when experienced later in the life cycle. We compared those respondents who had suffered from health problems since childhood or adolescence with respondents who had started experiencing health problems later in life. In the case of signing a petition, boycotting a product and expressing political opinions on social media, we found what was expected: those whose daily lives have been hampered by health problems since early age are significantly more active than those falling ill later in life (even after controlling for age). For other forms of participation, the opposite holds. These observations further complicate the overall picture of the health gap in participation: it is also the timing of the health problems that matters.

In Chapter 4, we turned to the analysis of political orientations, that is, attitudes towards the political system and towards the role of the self in the system. These orientations form the psychological context which either activates or demobilizes people to participate in politics. The results showed that health problems were connected to lower levels of political trust. People who have experience of poor health or disability tend to be less trustful towards political institutions and less satisfied with the way Finnish democracy is currently functioning. However, there was either no or only a slight health gap in the way that individuals understand politics or have any factual knowledge of political matters. A definite difference was found in terms of citizens' political identification: poor health tends to correlate positively with more left-leaning political identification.

Political participation does not take place in a vacuum. In Chapter 5, we looked at how the social context affects participation differences among people under varying health conditions. We tested how social connections, the level of social activity and health-related identity condition the relationship between health and participation. Although it would seem intuitive to think that the social environment will have an impact on how people with health problems behave politically, the analysis suggested only a limited effect. Social networks are conducive to political action, but mostly in the same way for people with and without health problems.

However, there were some exceptions. While there was no effect on turnout, for other forms of participation, the social context played a more important role for people with health concerns than for people who reported being healthy. Social ties thus seem particularly relevant for getting people engaged in politics beyond merely voting, with people whose lives are limited by disability especially needing the encouragement to mobilize through other forms of political participation. A supportive social context also seems to give people with a disability or long-term illness a greater sense of efficacy as well. Furthermore, those who identify with others with a health problem are much more likely to participate in health-related voluntary organizations, which suggests that identity plays a role in shaping the political behaviour of people with health problems.

As our data come from a single country, Finland, it is also important to evaluate our results in a comparative or international context. Furthermore, using comparative data enables an analysis of a highly relevant question, which is impossible to study in a single-country setting: how do institutional settings condition the association between health and participation? The results in Chapter 6 demonstrate that there is quite a large variation in the health-related participation gaps between individual countries. In countries such as Switzerland and Estonia, citizens with poor health are much less likely to vote in elections relative to those with good health. In other countries, however, being in a more difficult personal situation, healthwise, does not depress turnout as much. In the case of other forms of political participation, international comparisons show that health effects are substantially smaller.

Some institutional settings are more conducive to political mobilization among individuals with poor health, thus reducing the participation gap relative to healthy citizens. Four contextual factors were associated with lower turnout gaps between health groups in the empirical analysis: compulsory voting, party-centred electoral systems, higher trade union density and a greater share of left-wing parties. Compulsory voting more or less forces everybody to vote, including citizens who are generally less likely to participate. Party-centred electoral systems, involving fewer alternatives to consider, were more efficient at increasing turnout than candidate-centred systems. Mobilization is also important: turnout gaps between health groups were narrower in countries where trade union density is high. There were also some suggestions that turnout gaps are smaller in countries where the share of left-wing parties is high, even though the findings were not as robust as for other contextual variables.

Chapter 7 focused on preference differences, firstly, among health groups and, secondly, between these health groups and political elites. Overall, our results show that variation in health-related attitudes is more evident between citizens and candidates than between citizens in different health categories. Contradicting our initial expectation, differences in self-rated health (SRH) do not seem to be strongly connected to differences in attitudes. On issues concerning the current costs of healthcare and the provision of healthcare services by the public sector, both candidates and MPs are more aligned with healthier citizens. Voters with fair or poor health support public healthcare services and do not perceive the current healthcare costs as too expensive. All in all, there are some rather large preference differences, especially between those in poor health and MPs.

Hypotheses and theoretical considerations

Theoretically, we anchored our study into four traditions often used in the research field of political engagement. These traditions were discussed in Chapter 2 and, based on this discussion, we formulated seven hypotheses, which we tested in the empirical analysis. The theoretical traditions, and the hypotheses derived from them, were not thought to be mutually exclusive, but rather as complementing each other. Thus, our study was not a competition in which one of the theories would emerge as the winner. On the contrary, we think that using several theoretical approaches can deepen our understanding of the association between health and political engagement. Nevertheless, some theoretical expectations seemed to be more consistent with the results than others. In Table 8.2, we provide a summary of how these hypotheses were supported by the analyses.

Table 8.2 Summary of hypotheses and empirical support for them

HYPOTHESES	EMPIRICAL SUPPORT
Resource theory: *1. Poor health decreases political engagement.* *2. Poor health decreases political engagement to a lesser extent among people who have experienced health problems at least since childhood.*	Supported. In most cases poor health depresses engagement. Participation is less depressed among those with a longer history of health problems.
Self-interest theory: *3. Poor health increases political engagement.* *4. People with poor health and low socio-economic status have above-average rates of political engagement.*	Partial support. In some cases, health problems are associated with higher levels of participation (e.g., signing a petition, contacting decision makers). Poor health, combined with low socio-economic status, did not encourage participation.
Contextual theory: *5. Social connections are more important determinants of political engagement among people with health problems than among people in good health.*	Weak or no support. There were some, albeit weak and non-systematic, effects of social connections that mattered more for people with health problems.
Social identity theory: *6. Identifying with others who experience health problems increases the propensity for political engagement among people with health problems.* *7. Identifying with others who experience health problems increases the propensity for demanding forms of political engagement among people with health problems.*	Partial support. Health-related identity is connected to more active participation in patient organizations and voting, but not to other forms of participation. Patient organizations are also the only demanding form of participation for which we find a positive connection with health-related identity.

Resource theory, or some variant of it, is arguably the most common way to approach political participation (e.g. Smets and van Ham, 2013). There could be good reasons for this, as our analyses provided most support for hypotheses derived from this theory. Conceptually, we can think of health as either a resource that promotes participation or a factor that affects other resources (e.g., time available for participation, skills to be more efficient). However, the pertinent point here is that those with fewer health problems are usually more likely to vote and participate in other ways. That said, it is important to remember that there are important exceptions to this rule as well.

These exceptions can, at least to some extent, be explained by self-interest theory. In some cases, poor health encourages participation, such as signing petitions or contacting local officials or politicians. These forms of activities may originate from self-interested motivations. For example, having some chronic health conditions may stimulate individuals to contact public officials on personal matters related to healthcare services or financial subsidies associated with their condition. Unfortunately, our data do not allow us to differentiate respondents based on their motives to act politically. Another observation, which is consistent with the self-interest explanation, is related to political left-right identification. Those with impaired health are more likely to place themselves further to the left than those with no health problems, which could indicate that health worries lead to more support for leftist solutions, for example, in terms of welfare state support.

Contextual theories received less support than we perhaps originally anticipated. While social connections clearly matter for political participation, for the most part the effect seems to be equal to all, regardless of their health status. However, in some specific cases, it seems that good social relations are more conducive for those with health problems. Thus, there were some signs of support for contextual theory as well. Since, in this book, we are not able to delve into this question very deeply, we encourage others to study the effect of social context more carefully, as this question has clearly not yet been comprehensively dealt with.

Finally, our analyses lent some, albeit partial, support to identity theories. Health-related identity was connected to more active participation in patient organizations, but the effect on other forms of political participation was inconsistent or non-existent. However, we think that, with identity-related theories, the situation is similar to that of contextual theories: more analysis is needed.

Avenues for further research

The health–participation relationship is so complicated that it is impossible to cover it comprehensively in one study. As our aim was to provide a broad, general analysis of the field, many aspects were left untreated or dealt with only on a rather superficial level. Thus, a lot was left uncovered and undiscussed. However, we hope that this book serves as a starting point for more focused and detailed studies in the future. Next, we list some important avenues for further research, which could be especially fruitful in moving the field forward.

Causal relationships between health and political engagement: As explained in Chapter 2, the framework for this study was based on tentative ideas about the causal relationship between health-related social networks, identity and engagement. However, for the most part, we have tried to remain somewhat agnostic in terms of causality. Detecting and analyzing causal relationship require strong theories and specific kinds of data and methods, which were, as far as this book is concerned, outside of our reach. We, nevertheless, feel strongly that this is the way in which research on health and politics should proceed in the future.

Effect on close relatives and friends: Health problems, especially difficult ones, affect not only the individuals concerned, but also their social networks. Serious health conditions inevitably cause stress, worry and perhaps even financial troubles for family members, relatives and friends of the one affected by illness. While this effect is inevitably detectable in the case of caregivers of those with serious chronic conditions, the effect could radiate to other close ones as well. As far as we can tell, this area remains totally unexplored by researchers on the relationship between health and participation.

International comparisons and contextual effects: In Chapter 6, we provided a short cross-national comparison; given the available space, however, it was inevitably limited. We are strongly minded that more cross-national analyses are needed. We believe that, for the most part, our results are generalizable to other Western nations, although there is no denying that institutional settings or cultural factors will modify the effect between health and political engagement, probably in many ways. Furthermore, the health–participation relationship is largely unexplored in non-Western societies and developing countries.

Use of multiple indicators for health: Our results clearly show that the effect of health on participation is contingent on how health is defined and measured. The results suggest, for example, that the effect of health depends on whether one is suffering from a long-term condition or a more temporary illness. Timing also matters: the effect of health is different among those who have lived with a condition for a long time compared with those who have only been affected by health problems later in life. Furthermore, we know from other studies that the type of condition matters (Sund et al., 2017). Thus, we recommend, in addition to standard measures, such as the SRH question, the use of a wider variety of health indicators, which could take into account the complex and multidimensional nature of health problems. There are also several health-related quality-of-life measures, which can be used to gauge the general well-being of an individual in a more nuanced way than the simple SRH indicator (for example, the EuroQoL five-dimension quality of life measure; see Szende, Oppe and Devlin, 2007).

Final words: what to do with health-related inequalities in political engagement?

Throughout this book, we have demonstrated that health matters in terms of political engagement. Besides participation, political orientation and policy preferences are differentiated by an individual's health status. The effect of health on political engagement is not always negative; when it is, however, it poses a challenge for political equality. The obvious question, then, concerns how health-related inequalities in political engagement could be alleviated.

Echoing a growing awareness of negative consequences of economic, social and health inequalities, many researchers have been considering ways to enhance social justice. If there is enough political will, growing health inequalities can be tackled – for example, by active healthcare policies (e.g., Benach et al., 2013; Raphael, 2012). Nevertheless, in their recent contribution on social inequalities, Jensen and van Kersbergen (2017, p. 165) paint a gloomy vision: "[T]he trends that we observe today mostly point in the direction of increasing inequality – with all its adverse effects on health outcomes, social mobility and democratic participation." They also do not see any major social movements or political forces to counter these inegalitarian trends in the near future.

In relation to health and political equality, however, we are inclined to share a somewhat more optimistic view. The study of health effects on political participation is flourishing and rapidly growing. At the same time, the interpretation of political engagement is shifting from the framework of 'individual choice' to 'accessibility', i.e., from an emphasis on motivational factors to resources and facilitation (Wass and Blais, 2017). This change stems from the understanding that political engagement does not take place in a vacuum, but is closely connected to many aspects of life. Various types of inequalities, including differences in health, are thus often translated into differences in political engagement. On the other hand, such a connection suggests that policies tackling health inequalities may have positive implications for political inequality as well. As illustrated in this book, the mechanisms by which health is influencing political engagement are complex and cannot be affected by interventions that are only focused on the political system, such as electoral engineering (Norris, 2004). Instead, any intervention to tackle health-related political inequality should take a comprehensive approach, in which aspects of inclusive democracy are embedded in the planning and implementation processes in various policy fields.

References

Benach, J., Malmusi, D., Yasui, Y. and Martinez, J.M., 2013. A new typology of policies to tackle health inequalities and scenarios of impact based on Rose's population approach. *Journal of Epidemiology and Community Health*, 67(3), pp. 286–91.

Jensen, C. and van Kersbergen, K., 2017. *The politics of inequality*. London: Palgrave Macmillan.

Norris, P., 2004. *Electoral engineering: Voting rules and political behavior.* New York: Cambridge University Press.

Raphael, D., ed., 2012. *Tackling health inequalities: Lessons from international experiences*. Toronto: Canadian Scholars' Press Inc.

Sund, R., Lahtinen, H., Wass, H., Mattila, M. and Martikainen, P., 2016. How voter turnout varies between different chronic conditions? *Journal of Epidemiology and Community Health* 71(5), pp. 475–79.

Szende, A., Oppe, M. and Devlin, N., eds., 2007. *EQ-5D value sets: Inventory, comparative review and user guide*. Dordrecht: Springer.

Smets, K and van Ham, C., 2013. The embarrassment of riches? A meta-analysis of individual-level research on voter turnout. *Electoral Studies*, 32(2), pp. 344-59.

Wass, H. and Blais, A., 2017. Turnout. In K. Arzhaimer, J. Evans and M. Lewis-Beck, eds. *Sage Handbook of Electoral Behaviour*. London: Sage, pp. 459–87.

Appendix
Data sources

For the purposes of this book, we gathered new survey data on health and political engagement in Finland. These survey data have been used in our empirical analyses in Chapters 3 to 5 and 7. In the survey, 2,001 respondents were asked questions on an extensive variety of aspects relating to health and engagement. For example, in addition to 'standard' questions of political participation, we included several items that measure individuals' general health and specific types of possible health problems and disabilities they may have.

In the collection of the survey data, we took the problem of self-selection bias, caused, e.g., by refusals to take part in the survey and unknown telephone numbers, into account already before actually conducting the survey. In the first step, we asked the Population Register Centre of Finland to collect a random sample of 25,000 adult Finnish residents (aged 18 or over). Next, Statistics Finland linked these 25,000 individuals (using their personal identification codes) with several national data registers which include basic socio-economic data of Finnish citizens. With this linkage, we were able to obtain variables indicating, for example, gender, age, mother tongue, education, income and number of children among these 25,000 individuals.

In the next step, a telephone survey company collected telephone numbers for the 25,000 individuals in the sample. Because of confidential telephone numbers and unregistered pre-paid phones, correct telephone numbers were found for altogether 15,611 individuals. After that, the survey company contacted these persons randomly by phone to recruit them in the survey. This continued until the minimum number of 2,000 respondents was reached.

After the telephone survey data had been collected, we used the information obtained from the official registers to calculate appropriate weights for the 2,001 respondents. Using the original sample of 25,000, we calculated 'population' distributions for various socio-economic variables and used this information to calibrate the weights for respondents in the empirical analysis. In this process, we used a Stata programme called *ipfraking* (Kolenikov, 2014), which implements weight-calibration procedures known as iterative proportional fitting, or raking, of complex survey weights. To calculate the weights, we experimented with several sets of variables, but in the end selected the following variables, which produced the best match with the response and 'population' distributions:

- age group (18–34, 35–49, 50–64, 65–)
- marital status (unmarried, married or in a registered relationship, divorced, widowed)
- education (upper secondary education, short-cycle tertiary education, bachelor or equivalent level, master or equivalent level or higher)
- disposable income (divided into quintiles)
- home ownership status (owns home, renting, so-called ARAVA apartment, so-called ASO apartment, unknown).

In cross-national analyses in Chapter 6, the European Social Survey (ESS) and World Values Survey (WVS) were used. The European Social Survey is a centrally coordinated cross-national survey of social and political attitudes, covering over 30 countries during the 2000s and 2010s. ESS is collected via face-to-face interviews with representative samples of persons aged 15 and over, selected by random probability sampling methods. In Chapter 6, a cumulative data file, pooling data across six rounds of the ESS between 2002 and 2014, was combined with data from the seventh round (2014–2015). A total of 29 countries classified as 'free' according to the Freedom House Index were included in the analysis. Russia, Turkey, and Ukraine were rated as 'partly free' during the period and were consequently dropped from the analysis. In addition, we used data from the sixth wave of the World Values Survey, gathered between 2010 and 2014 in 54 countries. WVS is a world-wide study of values and their impact on social and political life. A select number of countries were analyzed in this chapter to account for health effects on voting in national and local elections.

The data sets used in Chapter 7 consist of candidates' responses in the Voting Advice Application by Finland's national public service broadcasting company, YLE. The candidates were given altogether 32 statements with four response categories: (1) completely agree, (2) completely disagree, (3) partly disagree and (4) completely disagree. Some statements were relevant only to a candidate's electoral district or did not cover the themes related to healthcare issues. Out of the altogether 32 statements, 5 were directly related to social and health policy and thus included in our survey conducted among the citizens. More information is provided by the Finnish Social Science Data Archive (FSD) in which the data set is deposited and publicly available for research purposes (https://services.fsd. uta.fi/catalogue/FSD3004?study_language=en).

Reference

Kolenikov, S., 2014. Calibrating survey data using iterative proportional fitting (raking). *The Stata Journal*, 14(1), pp. 22–59.

Index

www.ingramcontent.com/pod-product-compliance
Ingram Content Group UK Ltd.
Pitfield, Milton Keynes, MK11 3LW, UK
UKHW020348010325
455677UK00021B/340

9 780367 878436